Microsoft® Office
Access 2003

Level 1

Michael Sullivan

Microsoft® Office Access 2003: Level 1

Part Number: 084460
Course Edition: 1.1

ACKNOWLEDGMENTS

Project Team

Curriculum Developer and Technical Writer: Michael Sullivan • **Content Manager:** Cheryl Russo • **Content Editors:** Angie J. French, Christy D. Johnson and Laura Thomas • **Sr. Material Editors:** Lance Anderson, Elizabeth M. Fuller and Frank Wosnick • **Graphic Designer:** Julie Popken • **Project Technical Specialist:** Michael Toscano

NOTICES

HELP US IMPROVE OUR COURSEWARE

Your comments are important to us. Please contact us at Element K Press LLC, 1-800-478-7788, 500 Canal View Boulevard, Rochester, NY 14623, Attention: Product Planning, or through our Web site at **http://support.elementkcourseware.com**.

This logo means that this courseware has been approved by the Microsoft® Office Specialist Program to be among the finest available for learning Microsoft Access 2003. It also means that upon completion of this courseware, you may be prepared to take an exam for Microsoft Offices Specialist qualification.

What is a Microsoft Office Specialist? A Microsoft Office Specialist is an individual who has passed exams for certifying his or her skills in one or more of the Microsoft Office desktop applications such as Microsoft Word, Microsoft Excel, Microsoft PowerPoint, Microsoft Outlook, Microsoft Access, or Microsoft Project. The Microsoft Office Specialist Program typically offers certification exams at the "Core" and "Expert" skill levels. The Microsoft Office Specialist Program is the only program in the world approved by Microsoft for testing proficiency in Microsoft Office desktop applications and Microsoft Project. This testing program can be a valuable asset in any job search or career advancement.

To learn more about becoming a Microsoft Office Specialist, visit **www.microsoft.com/officespecialist**. To learn more about other Microsoft Office Specialist approved courseware from Element K, visit **www.elementkcourseware.com**.

*The availability of Microsoft Office Specialist certification exams varies by application, application version, and language. Visit **www.microsoft.com/officespecialist** for exam availability.

NOTES

MICROSOFT® OFFICE ACCESS 2003: LEVEL 1

LESSON 1: AN OVERVIEW OF ACCESS 2003

A. Understand Relational Databases **2**

    Database Terminology 2

B. Examine the Access Environment **5**

C. Open the Database Environment **8**

    Access Objects 8

    Naming Conventions 9

D. Examine an Access Table **12**

    Table Datasheet View 12

    Table Design View 13

LESSON 2: MANAGING DATA

A. Examine an Access Form **18**

    Forms 18

B. Add and Delete Records **22**

C. Sort Records **25**

D. Display Recordsets **27**

    Queries 27

E. Update Records **30**

F. Run a Report **33**

LESSON 3: ESTABLISHING TABLE RELATIONSHIPS

A. Identify Table Relationships **38**

B. Identify Primary and Foreign Keys in the Relationships Window **41**

    Primary Keys 41

    Foreign Keys 41

CONTENTS

C. Work with Subdatasheets **43**

Subdatasheets 43

LESSON 4: QUERYING THE DATABASE

A. Create a Select Query **50**

The Query Design Environment 50

B. Add Criteria to a Query **56**

Comparison Operators 56

Conditional Operators 56

C. Add a Calculated Field to a Query **61**

Arithmetic Operators 61

Access Expressions 61

The Expression Builder 62

D. Perform a Calculation on a Record Grouping **67**

LESSON 5: DESIGNING FORMS

A. Examine Form Design Guidelines **72**

AutoForms 72

The Form Wizard 73

B. Create a Form Using AutoForm **75**

C. Create a Form Using the Form Wizard **78**

D. Modify the Design of a Form **81**

Controls 82

Selecting Form Controls 82

Sizing Form Controls 85

Aligning and Spacing Form Controls 88

Moving Form Controls 89

LESSON 6: PRODUCING REPORTS

A. Create an AutoReport **96**

AutoReport 96

B. Create a Report by Using the Wizard **98**

The Report Wizard 98

C. Examine a Report in Design View **104**

Report Design View 104

D. Add a Calculated Field to a Report **107**

The Toolbox 107

E. Modify the Format Properties of a Control **110**

F. AutoFormat a Report **112**

G. Adjust the Width of a Report **114**

APPENDIX A: MICROSOFT OFFICE SPECIALIST PROGRAM

LESSON LABS **123**

SOLUTIONS **131**

GLOSSARY **139**

INDEX **141**

NOTES

ABOUT THIS COURSE

Most organizations maintain and manage large amounts of information. One of the most efficient and powerful information management computer applications is the relational database. Information can be stored, linked, and managed using a single relational database application and its associated tools. In this course, you will be introduced to the concept of the relational database by using the Microsoft® Office Access 2003 relational database application and its information management tools.

Managing large amounts of complex information is common in today's business environment and, if done properly, can provide any business an edge over the competition. However, mismanaged and lost information can cause you to fall behind. An implementation of the Access 2003 database application can give your business that positive edge.

Course Description

Target Student

This course is designed for students who wish to learn the basic operations of the Access 2003 database program to perform their day-to-day responsibilities, and to understand the advantages that using a relational database program can bring to their business processes. The Level 1 course is for the individual whose job responsibilities include working with tables to create and maintain records, locate records, and produce reports based on the information in the database. It also provides the fundamental knowledge and techniques needed to advance to more technical Access responsibilities, such as creating and maintaining new databases and using programming techniques that enhance Access applications.

Course Prerequisites

To ensure the successful completion of *Microsoft® Office Access 2003: Level 1,* we recommend completion of one of the following Element K courses, or equivalent knowledge from another source:

- *Windows 2000: Introduction*
- *Windows XP: Introduction*
- *Windows XP Professional: Level 1*
- *Windows XP Professional: Level 2*

How to Use This Book

As a Learning Guide

Each lesson covers one broad topic or set of related topics. Lessons are arranged in order of increasing proficiency with Access 2003; skills you acquire in one lesson are used and developed in subsequent lessons. For this reason, you should work through the lessons in sequence.

We organized each lesson into results-oriented topics. Topics include all the relevant and supporting information you need to master Access 2003, and activities allow you to apply this information to practical hands-on examples.

You get to try out each new skill on a specially prepared sample file. This saves you typing time and allows you to concentrate on the skill at hand. Through the use of sample files, hands-on activities, illustrations that give you feedback at crucial steps, and supporting background information, this book provides you with the foundation and structure to learn Access 2003 quickly and easily.

As a Review Tool

Any method of instruction is only as effective as the time and effort you are willing to invest in it. In addition, some of the information that you learn in class may not be important to you immediately, but it may become important later on. For this reason, we encourage you to spend some time reviewing the topics and activities after the course. For additional challenge when reviewing activities, try the "What You Do" column before looking at the "How You Do It" column.

As a Reference

The organization and layout of the book make it easy to use as a learning tool and as an after-class reference. You can use this book as a first source for definitions of terms, background information on given topics, and summaries of procedures.

This course is one of a series of Element K courseware titles that addresses Microsoft Office Specialist (Office Specialist) skill sets. The Office Specialist program is for individuals who use Microsoft's business desktop software and who seek recognition for their expertise with specific Microsoft products. Certification candidates must pass one or more proficiency exams in order to earn Office Specialist certification.

Course Objectives

In this course, you will be introduced to the features of the Access 2003 application.

You will:

- examine the Microsoft® Office Access 2003 database application.
- manage the data in a database.
- examine existing table relationships.
- query the database.
- design simple forms.

- create and modify Access reports.

Course Requirements

Hardware

For this course, you will need one computer for each student and one for the instructor. Each computer will need the following minimum hardware components:

- A 233 MHz Pentium-class processor if you use Windows XP Professional as your operating system. 300 MHz is recommended.
- A 133 MHz Pentium-class processor if you use Windows 2000 Professional as your operating system.
- 128 MB of RAM.
- A 6 GB hard disk.
- A floppy disk drive.
- A mouse or other pointing device.
- An 800 x 600–resolution monitor.
- Network cards and cabling for local network access.
- Internet access (see your local network administrator).
- A printer (optional).
- A projection system to display the instructor's computer screen.

Software

- Either Windows XP Professional with Service Pack 1, or Windows 2000 Professional with Service Pack 4.
- Microsoft® Office Professional Edition 2003.

Class Setup

For Initial Class Setup

1. Install Windows 2000 Professional or Windows XP Professional on an empty partition.
   - Leave the Administrator password blank.
   - For all other installation parameters, use values that are appropriate for your environment (see your local network administrator if you need details).
2. On Windows 2000 Professional, when the Network Identification Wizard runs after installation, select the Users Must Enter A User Name And Password To Use This Computer option. (This step ensures that students will be able to log on as the Administrator user regardless of what other user accounts exist on the computer.)
3. On Windows 2000 Professional, in the Getting Started With Windows 2000 dialog box, uncheck Show This Screen At Startup. Click Exit.

4. On Windows 2000 Professional, set 800 x 600 display resolution: Right-click the desktop and choose Properties. Select the Settings tab. Move the Screen Area slider to 800 By 600 Pixels. Click OK twice, and then click Yes.

5. On Windows 2000 Professional, install Service Pack 4. Use the Service Pack installation defaults.

6. On Windows XP Professional, disable the Welcome screen. (This step ensures that students will be able to log on as the Administrator user regardless of what other user accounts exist on the computer.) Click Start and choose Control Panel→User Accounts. Click Change The Way Users Log On And Off. Uncheck Use Welcome Screen. Click Apply Options.

7. On Windows XP Professional, install Service Pack 1. Use the Service Pack installation defaults.

8. On either operating system, install a printer driver (a physical print device is optional).

   • For Windows XP Professional, click Start and choose Printers And Faxes. Under Printer Tasks, click Add A Printer and follow the prompts.

   • For Windows 2000 Professional, click Start and choose Settings→Printers. Run the Add Printer Wizard and follow the prompts.

9. Run the Internet Connection Wizard to set up the Internet connection as appropriate for your environment if you did not do so during installation.

10. Log on to the computer as the Administrator user if you have not already done so.

11. Perform a Complete installation of Microsoft Office System, Version 2003.

12. Minimize the Language Bar if it appears.

13. Set the security level of Access 2003 to Low.

   a. Open Access 2003.

   b. Choose Tools→Macro→Security.

   c. Select the Low option.

   d. Click OK.

14. Install the Northwind.mdb sample database.

   a. Choose Help→Sample Databases.

   b. Follow the instructions for installation of the Northwind database.

   c. Close Access 2003.

15. On the course CD-ROM, open the 084_460 folder. Then, open the Data folder. Run the 084460dd.exe self-extracting file located within. This will install a folder named 084460Data on your C drive. This folder contains all the data files that you will use to complete this course. Copy all of the data files in the 084460Data folder and paste them into the My Documents folder.

Before Every Class

1. Log on to the computer as the Administrator user.

2. Delete any existing data files from the My Documents folder.

3. Extract a fresh copy of the course data files from the CD-ROM provided with the course manual. Copy all of the data files in the 084460Data folder and paste them into the My Documents folder.

List of Additional Files

Printed with each activity is a list of files students open to complete that activity. Many activities also require additional files that students do not open, but are needed to support the file(s) students are working with. These supporting files are included with the student data files on the course CD-ROM or data disk. Do not delete these files.

NOTES

LESSON 1

An Overview of Access 2003

Lesson Objectives:

In this lesson, you will examine the Microsoft® Office Access 2003 database application.

You will:

- Define the relational database concept.
- Examine the Access 2003 program environment.
- Examine an Access database's environment.
- Examine a table in an Access database.

Introduction

In most businesses, working with large amounts of varying types of data is a daily requirement. Understanding the composition of databases—and, in particular, the Access relational database program—will provide you with a foundation for using Microsoft® Office Access 2003 to organize your data. In this lesson, you will receive an introduction to database concepts, the Access database application environment, and an actual Access relational database.

With the Access relational database application installed in your business, you can organize and manage the data you have been tracking on paper. However, with an understanding of the relational database concept and the Access program, you will know where to begin. Identifying the features of a relational database, becoming familiar with the Access program, and opening and navigating through an Access database will provide you with the knowledge to begin managing your data.

TOPIC A

Understand Relational Databases

There are different types of databases, as well as applications that are sometimes mistakenly referred to as database programs. Understanding what a real database is and becoming familiar with the terms used to describe a database is the first step to becoming a competent database user. In this topic, you will be introduced to the relational database and the terminology that defines its components.

When an application, such as Access, is installed on your computer, it is very tempting to dive right in and start using the program. Gaining an understanding of the application you are about to use and being versed in its terminology is a much better starting point.

Database Terminology

Like many other computer programs, database applications have their own language. A few of the most common terms are listed in the following table.

Term	Meaning
Table	A group of records stored in rows and columns.
Record	A set of data about one person or thing.
Field	A category of information that pertains to all records.
Value	A single piece of data.

Relational Databases

Definition:

Simply put, a *database* is a collection of information. A *relational database* takes that concept one step further. A relational database is a file that stores information in multiple tables. Each table stores one specific category of information. The relational database can access these tables and extract, reorganize, and display the information contained within them in many different ways without altering the original table structures.

A relational database offers several benefits:

- Flexbility
- Simplicity
- Ease of management
- Power

Example:

A travel agent maintains two client tables. The first table contains information on the time of year clients prefer to travel, while the second table contains data on the clients' favorite vacation spots. Using a relational database, the travel agent can produce a report listing their customers' favorite vacation spots and the time of year they prefer to travel. The report can be used to send promotions to clients at appropriate times. All of this is accomplished without altering the original tables.

Temperatures in Fahrenheit				
City	May	June	July	August
Madrid	79	84	88	94
New York	62	73	82	84
Tehran	65	74	77	84
Hong Kong	72	78	88	93
Sidney	42	40	37	34
Tokyo	59	65	75	82

Temperatures in Fahrenheit			
Customer ID	Customer Name	Favorite City	Preferred Travel Month
0610	Mr. Velasco	Mexico City	September
0611	Ms. Sands	Florence	June
0612	Mr. and Mrs. Worthington	Madrid	May
0613	Mr. Beljima	Hong Hong	August
0614	Mr. and Mrs. Alexander	San Tropez	July
0615	Mr. and Mrs. Togarth	Orlando	May

Dear Mr. and Mrs. Worthington,
We at Adventures Abound Travel hope this letter finds you healthy in the New Year. We wanted to inform you that the temperature in Madrid for May is projected to be in the high 70s with sunny skies and this may be a great choice for your annual spring vacation.

Fiestas de San Isidro which honors the patron saint of Madrid, will be taking place on May 15. This festival is the city's most lively and popular event of the year. Please give me a call at 778-3824 to get more details and to make reservations to hold a spot for you in first class on Iberia Airways.

Sincerely,
Joanie Vassar
Adventures Abound Travel

Figure 1-1: *The relational database.*

ACTIVITY 1-1

Identifying a Relational Database

Activity Time:

5 minutes

Scenario:

You are attempting to understand what a database is and how it works, and to be more precise, what a relational database is and how it differs from other database types. Reviewing examples and characteristics of databases, particularly relational databases, will help you understand these concepts.

What You Do	How You Do It

1. **What are some examples of collections of data that you use in your personal life?**

2. **What are some examples of collections of data that you use in your job?**

3. **Which of the following is representative of a relational database?**

   a) Note card

   b) Library file system

   c) Index in a book

   d) Glossary in a book

4. **Which of the following is *not* an advantage of the relational database?**

   a) Flexibility

   b) Simplicity

   c) Redundancy

   d) Ease of management

   e) Power

TOPIC B

Examine the Access Environment

Now that you are familiar with the concept of a relational database, it is time to take a look at the application you will be using. In this topic, you will launch the Access program and examine the environment used to create new Access database files and interface with existing ones.

When you launch Access, you have not yet opened a real database; you've only opened the interface that allows you to create new databases and open and manage existing databases. This is much like entering a house without knowing how to open any of the doors to the rooms. Unless you understand how to open and close the database files that hold your information, your relationship to the database is extremely limited. An understanding of the interface that performs these actions is essential to managing your information.

Access Environment Components

The Access 2003 environment enables you to open existing databases and create new databases. There are three primary components of the application environment:

- The menu bar is where commands are displayed and executed.
- The toolbar is a row of *icons* used to execute commands.
- The task pane is where you can search for files and consult the Microsoft Office online product information.

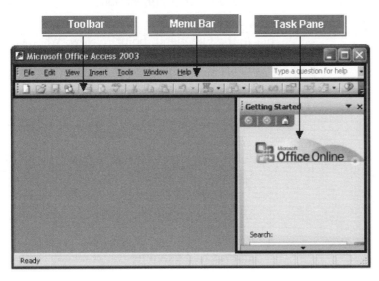

Figure 1-2: *The Access 2003 application environment.*

ACTIVITY 1-2

Examining the Access Environment

Activity Time:

10 minutes

Scenario:

Access is installed on your computer. It's now time to launch the application and explore its basic features.

What You Do	How You Do It
1. **Launch Access.**	a. From the Start menu, **choose All Programs→Microsoft Office→Microsoft Office Access 2003.**
	In Windows 2000, choose Start→Programs→ Microsoft Access.
2. **Examine the menus on the menu bar.**	a. On the menu bar, **click File** to display the File menu. The commands are similar to those in other applications.
	b. In the File menu, **point to New.** When you point to an active command, Access highlights the command.
	c. In the File menu, **point to Close.** Because this command is inactive, nothing happens when you point to it.
	Inactive items appear grayed out in all of the menus.
	d. On the menu bar, **display the other menus and examine the choices.**
	e. **Click a blank area of the screen** to close the open menu.

3. In the Access application, **use the tooltips to examine the tools on the toolbar.**

   a. On the toolbar, **hover the mouse pointer over the first button on the left** to display the tooltip.

      > Inactive buttons appear grayed out, as did the inactive menu items.

   b. Moving from left to right, **display the tooltip for each button.**

4. **By default, which of the following toolbar options are activated when you launch the Access application?**

   a) New

   b) Open

   c) Save

   d) Cut

   e) Microsoft Office Access Help

   f) Undo

   g) Code

   h) File Search

5. **Navigate through the available task panes.**

   a. On the toolbar, **click the File Search button** to display the Basic File Search task pane in which you can search for a database file.

   b. In the task pane's navigation bar, **click the Home button** to return to the Getting Started task pane.

   c. **Click the Back button** to return to the Basic File Search task pane.

   d. On the toolbar, **click the New button** to display the New File task pane.

   e. In the task pane's navigation bar, **click the Back button** to display the Basic File Search task pane again.

   f. **Click the Forward button** to display the New File task pane.

   g. **Click the Home button** to display the Getting Started task pane.

TOPIC C

Open the Database Environment

You have opened the Access application and looked at a few of its most basic features. In this topic, you will open an Access database and identify the components that make up the database.

It is, of course, important to understand the relational database concept and the interface that appears when you launch the Access program. You must also be familiar with the database file structure within Access. Doing so will allow you to open the files that hold your data and employ the tools to manage it.

Access Objects

The Database window displays the Access objects in the left pane. Access objects are the tools that are used to store and work with your data.

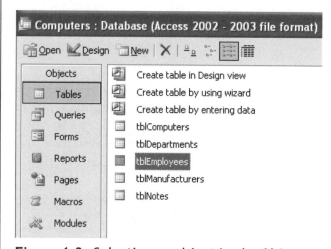

Figure 1-3: *Selecting an object in the Objects pane on the left side of the Database window allows you to view all instances of that Access object within the database file.*

Although the Objects pane does contain seven Access objects, for the purposes of this course you will only be concerned with the top four. The following table provides a brief description of the objects that will be used in this course.

Object	Description
Tables	Storage container for the data.
Queries	Question that retrieves data from tables. Queries may be saved for reuse. Queries always display either record level output (list format) or summary information (a query cannot display both detail and summary).
Forms	Graphical interface used for data entry and/or displaying data and other objects.
Reports	Screen output of data arranged in an order specified by the user.

Naming Conventions

Naming conventions are sets of rules that can be applied to Access objects in order to identify them. The rules call for a unique prefix to be assigned to the beginning of an object name.

Common Applications of Naming Conventions

Some, but not all developers use naming conventions at the field level. The two most common naming conventions are the Leszynski naming convention and the Reddick naming convention. Naming conventions are optional and the type of naming convention utilized is strictly up to the user. The following table illustrates examples of commonly used naming conventions.

Object	Prefix	Example
Table	tbl	tblSampleTable
Select Queries	qry	qrySampleQuery or qryselSampleQuery
Forms	frm	frmSampleForm
Subforms	fsub	fsubSampleSubform
Reports	rpt	rptSampleReport
Subreports	rsub	rsubSampleSubReport

How to Open and View an Access Database

Procedure Reference: Open and View a Database

To open and view a database:

1. Start Access.

2. Locate the database files.

3. Select the database file to open.

4. Click Open.

You could also double-click a database file to open it.

ACTIVITY 1-3

Opening and Viewing an Access Database

Activity Time:

5 minutes

Data Files:

- Computers.mdb

Setup:

Access is running. No files are open.

Scenario:

A consultant has created an inventory database, Computers.mdb, containing information on all of the organization's computers, including who uses them, in which department they are used, their manufacturer, their price, whether they are under warranty, and their tracking number. By opening the database and viewing the data it contains, you hope to gain a better understanding of the company's computer inventory.

What You Do	How You Do It
1. In the Computers.mdb database, in the Objects pane, **verify that the Tables object is highlighted and examine the table objects.**	a. On the Getting Started task pane, **click the Open link.**
	b. From the My Documents folder, **locate and double-click Computers.mdb** to open the database and display the Database window.
	c. **Examine the Objects pane on the left side of the Computers Database window.**
	d. If necessary, in the Objects pane, **click Tables** to display the table objects.

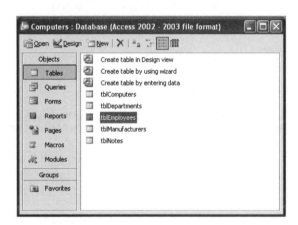

	e. In the right pane, **examine the list of objects.** At the top of the list are the tools to create tables, followed by the list of existing tables in the Computers.mdb database.
2. **Display the queries, forms, and reports in the Computers.mdb database.**	a. In the Objects pane, **select Queries.** The right pane displays a list of query creation tools and queries stored in the Computers. mdb database.
	b. In the Objects pane, **select Forms.** The right pane changes to display a list of form creation tools and the forms stored in the database.
	c. In the Objects pane, **select Reports.** The right pane displays report creation tools and a report stored in the database.

3. In the left pane, **collapse and expand the Objects listing.**

> Groups is an advanced feature discussed in a future course.

   a. In the left pane, **click Groups** to collapse the Objects listing.

   b. **Click Objects** to expand the listing again.

4. **Match the type of Access object with the description of the function(s) that it performs.**

___ report	a.	Displays data for editing.
___ table	b.	Arranges data for printed output.
___ query	c.	Displays selected data.
___ form	d.	Stores data on a single topic.

TOPIC D

Examine an Access Table

You have toured the Access interface and viewed an MDB database file where your information, and the Access objects used to manage it, are stored. Now you will open an Access table to view some of the data that populates the database.

Understanding the application interface and the structure of the database files is like knowing the directions to a bank and how the safe deposit boxes are organized. It is essential to know, but not very useful unless you know how to open the safe deposit boxes and access the valuables. Opening an Access table that contains your information and using the Access program's views to work with the tables is like having the keys to the safe deposit boxes.

Table Datasheet View

Datasheet view is the default view a user sees when opening a table or using a query. The data is arranged in rows and columns and the format resembles an Excel worksheet.

In Datasheet view:

- Record selectors appear to the left of each record, allowing users to select an entire record to copy or delete.
- A navigation bar allows the user to navigate to a specific record.

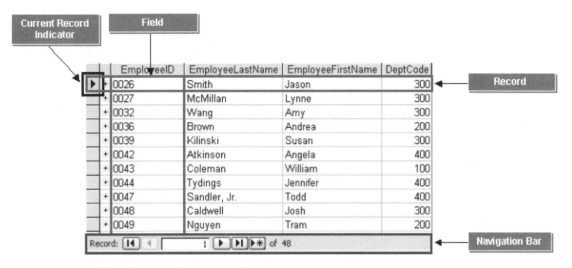

Figure 1-4: *Table displayed in Datasheet view.*

Table Design View

Design view is displayed when the user clicks the View button when a table is open in Datasheet view. In Design view, the user is looking at the components that make up the table from a developer's perspective. Field names, *data types*, and field properties are set, defined, and described within the Design view.

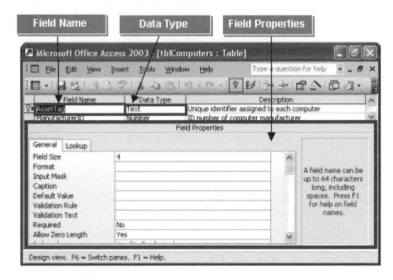

Figure 1-5: *Table displayed in Design view.*

Working with an Access Table in Datasheet and Design Views

Datasheet view allows you to work with the data in a table, while Design view allows you to modify the appearance and manner in which the form operates. It is not possible for an individual user of a single database to work with a table in Datasheet view and, simultaneously, to open the same table in Design view.

ACTIVITY 1-4

Comparing Datasheet and Design Views of an Access Table

Activity Time:

10 minutes

Setup:

Computers.mdb is open.

Scenario:

Knowing that there are different ways to view a table, you would like to obtain a better understanding of the differences between those views. By viewing the tblEmployees table in Datasheet view and then in Design view, you can see the differences.

What You Do	How You Do It
1. Open the tblEmployees table.	a. In the Database window, with Tables selected, **double-click tblEmployees.**

2. Using the Tab and arrow keys, the mouse pointer, and the table's navigation bar, **move through the tblEmployees table.**

   a. **Press the Tab key three times** to move through the fields in the table.

   b. **Hold down the Shift key and press Tab three times** to move back through the fields.

   c. **Press the arrow keys** to move around the fields in the table.

   d. **Click the record selector (the gray left column) of EmployeeID 0036** to select Andrea Brown's entire record.

   e. In the Record Navigation bar at the bottom of the table, **click the First Record button** [◄] to select the first record in the table.

   f. In the Record Navigation bar, **click the Next Record button** [►] to select the second record in the table.

   g. In the Record Navigation bar, **click the Last Record button** [►|] to select the last record in the table, Edward Bernstein's record.

3. **Display the tblEmployees table in Design view and examine the properties of the EmployeeID field.**

   a. On the far left of the table datasheet's toolbar, **click the View button** [ ] to display the tblEmployees table in Design view.

   b. **Click the table window's Maximize button** to maximize the display.

   c. **Press the down arrow** to move to the next field and observe the change in the properties in the lower panel.

   d. **Press the down arrow again** to move to the next fields and observe the properties in the lower panel.

   e. **Press the down arrow a final time** to move to the last field and observe the properties in the lower panel.

   f. In the upper pane, **select the EmployeeID field.**

4. **What is the data type of the EmployeeID field in tblEmployees?**

   a) Currency

   b) Date

   c) Number

   d) Text

5. **What is the data type of the DeptCode field in the tblEmployees table?**

   a) Currency

   b) Date

   c) Number

   d) Text

6. **What is the field size of EmployeeID?**

   a) 2 characters

   b) 4 characters

   c) 20 characters

   d) 20 digits

7. **Close the table and database.**

   a. **Choose File→Close** to close the table.

   b. **Choose File→Close** to close the database.

Lesson 1 Follow-up

In this lesson, you were introduced to the composition of databases and the Access relational database program. In addition, you opened and briefly examined the Access database application environment and an Access relational database.

1. **Why is it important to understand the way the database objects interact?**

2. **What kinds of information do you plan to build databases for?**

LESSON 2
Managing Data

Lesson Objectives:

In this lesson, you will manage the data in a database.

You will:

- Examine an Access 2003 form.
- Add and delete records from a table.
- Use different criteria to sort the records in a table.
- Use Select queries to display recordsets.
- Update the records in a table by working in the table, by using a form, and then by using a query.
- Run a report to display a table's records in a report format.

Introduction

Understanding the Access environment is the first step in managing the information in the database. Knowing how to use the data management tools that are provided with the application is the next step. In this lesson, you will work directly within a table to manage the table's data, then move out of the table and use forms, queries, and reports to indirectly manage the same data.

The most important component of a relational database is the table, where your information is stored. Knowing how to use the other components of a database will allow you to reap the benefits of your database and ensure that you have more time to spend on your other responsibilities.

TOPIC A

Examine an Access Form

Now that you have worked in the Access environment, it is time to begin using the data management objects provided by Access. In this topic, you will examine an Access form, an object that allows you to locate and manage individual records.

You have opened, examined, and toured a table. Now, imagine a table with thousands of records and each record containing multiple fields. Moving about the table to locate and modify a single field in an individual record could be a challenging task. The Access form object simplifies the process by allowing you to manage data through a graphical user interface.

Forms

Definition:

An Access *form* is the object that is used to display, add, delete, and edit data in a table.

When using a form, keep in mind that:

- The data is never stored in the form, the form only displays the data stored in the table.
- Forms can be based on a table or a query.
- Forms can be viewed in one of three ways: Datasheet view, Design view, or Form view.
- In addition to displaying table data, forms can include calculations, graphics, and other objects.

Example:

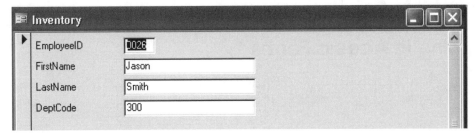

Figure 2-1: *A sample form.*

Navigation in an Access Form

In a form, the navigation bar at the bottom of the form is an easy method of moving from one record to another. The current record number, the record whose data is currently displayed in the form, is indicated in the navigation bar. The buttons on the navigation bar are used to move forward and backward through the records in the table. To move through the data displayed in the form, you can use the mouse or the keys and keystroke combinations found in the following table.

Keystroke	Movement
Tab, Enter, right arrow, down arrow	Pressing Tab or Enter, or the right or down arrow, moves you to the next field in the form. If it is the last field in the form, it moves you to the first field of the next record.
Shift+Tab, left arrow, up arrow	Pressing Shift+Tab, or the left arrow or up arrow, will move you to the previous field in the form. If it is the first field in the form, it moves you to the last field of the previous record.
Page Up	Pressing Page Up will move you to the same field in the previous record. (This will only work if the form is built properly.)
Page Down	Pressing Page Down will move you to the same field in the next record. (This will only work if the form is built properly.)
Home	Pressing Home will move you to the first field of the record you are currently in.
End	Pressing End will move you to the last field of the record you are currently in.
Ctrl+Home	Pressing Ctrl+Home will move you to the first field in the first record of the table with which you are working.
Ctrl+End	Pressing Ctrl+End will move you to the last field in the last record of the table with which you are working.

ACTIVITY 2-1

Navigating in Access Forms

Activity Time:

5 minutes

Data Files:

• UseForms.mdb

Scenario:

Your manager has suggested you look at some forms in the UseForms.mdb database so you can get an understanding of how they appear, how they are used, and what format best suits the company's needs.

What You Do	How You Do It
1. On the toolbar, **click the File Search button and,** in the task pane, **open the UseForms.mdb database, then open the frmCustomers form.**	a. On the toolbar, **click the File Search button.**
	b. In the Basic File Search task pane's Search Text text box, **type *UseForms.mdb***
	c. **Click Go.**
	d. When the UseForms.mdb file list appears, **determine which file is in My Documents then click the My Documents\ UseForms.mdb file.**
	e. **Close the Search Results task pane.**
	f. In the Objects pane, **select Forms.**
	g. In the Database window's right pane, **double-click frmCustomers** to open the form and display the first record in the tblCustomers table.
2. How many fields are displayed in the form?	
3. What field is highlighted by default?	

4. How many records are in the table?

5. Move through the record's fields, to the next record, and then return to the first record in the table.

    a. With the CustomerID field selected, **press the Tab key** to move to the CustomerName field.

    b. **Press the Tab key until the Postal Code field is selected.**

    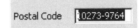

    Postal Code 00273-9764

    c. **Press the Tab key one more time** to move to the second record in the tblCustomer table.

    d. **Press Shift+Tab** to move back to the first record in the tblCustomers table.

    e. Using the Shift+Tab key combination, **move to record number one's Fax field.**

6. Move to the first field in the record and then to the last field in the record.

    a. With the Fax field of the first record selected, **press Home** to move to the CustomerID field.

    b. **Press End** to move to the last field of the record, Postal Code.

7. Move to the last field in the last record, move to the Fax field of the last record, and then return to the first field in the first record.

    a. With the last field of the first record selected, **press Ctrl+End** to move to the last field in the last record in the table.

    b. **Press Shift+Tab** to move to the Fax field in the last record.

    c. With the Fax field of the last record selected, **press Ctrl+Home** to return to the first field in the first record.

8. Using the navigation bar, **move to the second record in the table, the last record, the next-to-last record, and then return to the first record in the table.**

a. With Record 1 displayed, in the navigation bar located at the bottom of the form, **click the Next Record button** to move to the second record.

b. In the navigation bar, **click the Last Record button** to move to Record 14, the last record.

c. While located in the last record, **click the Previous Record button** ◄ to move to Record 13.

d. **Click the First Record button** to return to Record 1.

TOPIC B

Add and Delete Records

Two of the most commonly performed database operations are the addition and deletion of information. Generally, these are ongoing operations that are performed on a regular basis. In this topic, you will add new records to a table and delete existing records from a table.

Having current information in your database is one of the most important qualities of a database. A database that is incomplete or that contains outdated records is not a reliable source of information. By conscientiously adding new records and deleting old ones, your table will provide reliable, up-to-the-moment information. It will also prevent the database from becoming outdated.

How to Add and Delete Records

Procedure Reference: Add a Record to a Table

To add a record and enter the data:

1. On the table's navigation bar, click the New Record button.

2. Enter the new record data.

3. Press Enter to accept the new record.

Procedure Reference: Delete a Record from a Table

To delete a record:

1. Select the record to be deleted.

2. Either press Delete or choose Edit→Delete.

ACTIVITY 2-2

Adding and Deleting Records in a Table

Activity Time:

10 minutes

Setup:

The UseForms.mdb database is open and the frmCustomers form is displayed on the screen.

Scenario:

Adding and deleting records is going to be part of your daily routine and you would like to determine the most efficient method to complete those operations. By trying several techniques with the tblCustomers table, you can determine the most efficient method.

What You Do	How You Do It
1. Add a new customer record to the table.	a. In the frmCustomers form's navigation bar, **click the New Record button** ▶✱ to clear the form in preparation for entry of a new record.
	b. In the blank form, **enter the following data:**
	• CustomerID: 21998
	• CustomerName: Brave New Shoppers
	• Phone: (456) 777-6668
	• Fax: (456) 777-6669
	• Address: 39 Rosey Blvd.
	• City: Camptown
	• Region: NY
	• Country: US
	• Postal Code: 13355-0000
	c. **Close the form.**
2. Display tblCustomers and view the new record.	a. **Display tblCustomers and locate the new record.**

3. How many records are in the table?

    a) 12

    b) 13

    c) 14

    d) 15

4.	Delete the Household Helper record.	a.	In tblCustomers, **verify that the right pointing Current Record Indicator is located in the first record, Household Helper.**
		b.	**Choose Edit→Select Record** to highlight the Household Helper record.
		c.	**Choose Edit→Delete.**
		d.	When prompted to verify the record deletion, **click Yes** to complete the operation.

5.	**Use the navigation bar to add a new record to the table.**	a.	In the tblCustomers table's navigation bar, **click the New Record button.**
		b.	**Enter the following data:**
			• CustomerID: 21999
			• CustomerName: Super Savers
			• Address: 3669 Windy Way
			• City: Coalville
			• Region: UT
			• Country: US
			• Postal Code: 13365-0000
			• Phone: (454) 888-6668
			• Fax: (454) 888-6667

6.	**Close the table and the database.**	a.	**Close tblCustomers and the UseForms database.**

TOPIC C

Sort Records

You have been asked to locate all of the individuals in a specific department who are listed in a large table in which the records have been entered over a long period of time. The records you need to find are located throughout the table. In this topic, you will use several techniques to order the table's data and locate the desired records.

Viewing and locating specific records in a large table can be difficult and time-consuming. To simplify the process and reduce the time you spend searching, Access provides you with several techniques to assist you in sorting and locating the desired records.

How to Sort Records

Procedure Reference: Sort Records in a Table

To sort the records in a table:

1. In the Database window, select Tables.

2. Open the table you wish to sort.

3. In the table, select a field in the column by which you wish to sort the table.

4. Sort the table:
   - From the toolbar, select either the Sort Ascending or Sort Descending option;
   - Or, choose either Records→Sort→Sort Ascending or Records→Sort→Sort Descending.

ACTIVITY 2-3

Sorting Records in a Table

Activity Time:

10 minutes

Data Files:

- SampleTables.mdb

Scenario:

Your sales manager has learned that you have an abundance of information available at your fingertips in the database and she would like to take advantage of it. She would like to know how many orders in the tblCustomers table of the SampleTables.mdb database have been placed by Zilinski's Home Store and how many have been placed by Household Helper. With the Access sorting tools, you'll accomplish this task in no time.

LESSON 2

What You Do	How You Do It
1. From the SampleTables.mdb database, **open the tblCustomers table.**	a. **Open the SampleTables.mdb database.**
	b. **Open tblCustomers.**

2. **Locate the CustomerID numbers for Household Helper and Zilinski's Home Store.**	a. Locate the Household Helper record and **record the CustomerID number** _____. (It is the lowest number in the table.)	
	b. Locate the Zilinski's Home Store record and **record the CustomerID number** _____. (It is the highest number in the database).	
	c. **Close the table.**	

3. **Open tblOrders.**	a. **Open tblOrders.**

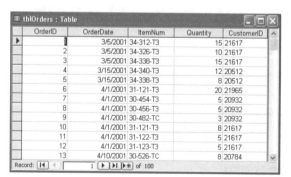

4. **How is the table sorted?**

  a) By OrderID

  b) By ItemNum

  c) By Quantity

5. Sort the table in ascending order, displaying the Household Helper orders at the top of the table.	a. With the tblOrders table displayed, **place the insertion point in the first field in the CustomerID column.**
	b. **Choose Records→Sort→Sort Ascending.** Examine the results; there are three Household Helper orders at the top of the list.
6. Sort the table in descending order, displaying Zilinski's orders at the top of the table.	a. With the tblOrders table displayed, **place the insertion point in the first field in the CustomerID column.**
	b. **Choose Records→Sort→Sort Descending.** There are 10 Zilinski's Home Store orders at the top of the list.
7. Sort the OrderID column in ascending order.	a. **Click in any field in the OrderID column.**
	b. **Click the Sort Ascending button on the toolbar** to sort the OrderID column in ascending order, restoring it to its original state.

TOPIC D

Display Recordsets

Sorting the records in a table in ascending or descending order, based on the values in a field, is a very useful operation. However, there are times when you need to extract groups of related records, such as records with the same department name or range of values. In this topic, you will use the Access query object to locate and display record groupings that meet a specific criteria.

You have been asked to locate all employees whose pay rate is between $12.50 and $15.00 per hour in a table that has several thousand records. You know that doing this in a table's Datasheet view will take longer than you have been given and there is a good chance you would miss some. By using a query, which searches the table for records with values in this range, you can accomplish the task more quickly and accurately.

Queries

Definition:

A *query* displays data from one or more tables in an ordered manner, as defined by the query's developer.

Example:

A valid query is a query that is located in the Queries list in the Database window. Its name may begin with the qry *prefix*, but that is not a requirement. When selected and launched or double-clicked, it is set into action and the results of the query are displayed.

How to Display Sets of Records

Procedure Reference: Display Sets of Records

To display a recordset:

1. In the Database window, select Tables.

2. Open the table you wish to sort.

3. In the table, locate and select a single occurrence of the value you wish to find.

4. Display the recordset:
   - On the toolbar, click the Filter By Selection button;
   - Or, choose Records→Filter→Filter By Selection.

Procedure Reference: Remove a Filter

To remove the filter:

1. Either click the toolbar's Remove Filter button or choose Records→Remove Filter/Sort.

ACTIVITY 2-4

Displaying Sets of Records

Activity Time:

10 minutes

Setup:

The SampleTables.mdb database is open and the tblOrders table is displayed.

Scenario:

The Sales Managers would like a printout of only Zilinski's Home Store orders and a printout of only the Household Helper orders. Using the sorting tools, you can group the orders together, but not pull them out of the table. Fortunately, the consultant who implemented your application built a simple Select query to display the orders for Household Helper. So, by using the Filter By Selection tool, you can display only the orders for each customer.

What You Do	How You Do It
1. Use the Filter By Selection tool to display the Household Helper order recordset, and then view it in Print Preview.	a. In the CustomerID column, **place the insertion point in any field with a 20151 value.** This is the Household Helper Customer ID number. b. From the toolbar, **click the Filter By Selection button** to display the recordset of Household Helper orders.

tblOrders : Table				
OrderID	OrderDate	ItemNum	Quantity	CustomerID
37	6/14/2001	30-352-TC	15	20151
38	6/14/2001	30-526-TC	6	20151
76	10/4/2001	30-452-T3	5	20151
(AutoNumber)	3/18/2003		0	

Record: 1 of 3 (Filtered)

What You Do	How You Do It
2. **Use Print Preview to view the Household Helper recordset.** Then, **close the Preview window and use the Remove Filter tool to close the recordset.**	a. On the toolbar, **click the Print Preview button** to preview how the printed recordset would appear. b. Using the Zoom feature, **click in the preview** to enlarge the display. c. **Press Esc** to close the Print Preview window and return to the table. d. On the toolbar, **click the Remove Filter button** to close the recordset display and return to the tblOrders table.
3. **Locate one of the Zilinski's Home Stores CustomerID fields and apply a filter** to display the recordset of their orders.	a. In the CustomerID column, **place the insertion point in any field with a 21965 value.** This is the Zilinski's Home Stores Customer ID number. b. From the menu, **choose Records→ Filter→Filter By Selection** to display the recordset of Zilinski Home Stores orders.
4. **Use Print Preview to display the Zilinski's Home Stores recordset.** Then, **close the Print Preview window and remove the filter** to close the recordset and return to the tblOrders table.	a. **Choose File→Print Preview and size the display to the screen** to preview how the printed page would appear. b. **Press Esc** to close the Print Preview window. c. **Choose Records→Remove Filter/Sort** to view all the records.

Lesson 2: Managing Data

5. Close the open table without saving, display the Queries objects, and select the qryHouseholdHelperOrders query.

a. Close the tblOrders table. Click No when prompted to save the changes.

b. With the SampleTables Database window open, in the Objects pane, **select Queries** to display any existing queries.

c. **Examine the right pane and verify that the qryHouseholdHelperOrders query is present.**

d. In the right pane, **double-click the qryHouseholdHelperOrders query** to run the query and display the recordset of Household Helper orders. You will notice that it was not necessary for any of the tables to be open when the query was run.

e. **Close the recordset.**

TOPIC E

Update Records

In the previous topics, you used a form to view data and a filter to display specific data. In this topic, you will use the form and query objects together to locate, edit, and update the records in a table that meet specific criteria.

There is little doubt that you will be continually changing and updating records in your database. The more efficiently you can perform operations, the more time you will have for other responsibilities. By using a query and a form in combination, you will be able to quickly locate the records you need and, when possible, display them in edit mode.

How to Update Records

Procedure Reference: Update Records

To update a record:

1. In the Database window, in the Objects pane, select Tables.

2. From the list of tables, open the table you wish to update.

3. Locate the field with the information that requires updating.

4. Select the value of this field and modify the data.

5. Press the down arrow or Enter to accept the changes.

6.   Close the table.

ACTIVITY 2-5

Updating Records

Activity Time:

10 minutes

Setup:

The SampleTables.mdb database is open.

Scenario:

Your manager has asked you to make several updates to the tblEmployees table in the SampleTables.mdb database. These include name, phone number, and ZIP Code changes. This is your first attempt at editing fields in a table and there are several editing techniques you can use. By trying several, you can determine which work best for you.

What You Do	How You Do It
1. In the tblEmployees table, **change Shelly Griffith's ZIP Code from 72308 to 99336.**	a. **Open and maximize the tblEmployees table.**
	b. **Click in the EmployeeID field with a value of 0057.** This is Shelly Griffith's record.
	c. **Press Tab six times** to highlight the ZIP Code.
	d. With the ZIP Code selected, **type 99336**
	🖈 Notice that the Current Record Indicator to the far left changes to a pencil 🖉 .
	e. **Press the down arrow.** The Record Indicator returns to its original state and the change is accepted.

2. **Locate Employee ID Number 0078, and correct the spelling of the name to Ballantine.**

   a. In the EmployeeID column, **locate EmployeeID 0078.** This is Carl Ballantyne's record.

   b. **Click between the "t" and the "y" in Ballantyne.**

   c. **Type *i* and delete the "y"** to change Ballantyne to Ballantine.

   d. **Press the down arrow** to accept the edit.

3. **Change Lisa Fitzpatrick's phone number from (607) 555-3310 to (585) 555-5595.**

   a. **Position the insertion point in any field in the LastName column.**

   b. **Choose Edit→Find** to display the Find And Replace dialog box.

   c. **Verify that the following criteria are selected:**
   - Look In: LastName
   - Match: Whole Field
   - Search: All

   d. In the Find What text box, **type *Fitzpatrick* and then click Find Next** to locate Lisa Fitzpatrick's record.

   e. **Click Cancel** to close the Find And Replace dialog box.

   f. With the insertion point located in Lisa Fitzpatrick's record, **press Tab six times to the HomePhone field and change the value to *(585) 555-5595***

   g. **Press the down arrow** to accept the change.

4. Use the Find And Replace option to change Lisa Fitzpatrick's last name to Fitzgerald and close the database.

a. Position the insertion point in the LastName column.

b. On the toolbar, **click the Find button** 🔍 to launch the Find And Replace Dialog Box. **Select the Replace tab.**

c. With Fitzpatrick in the Find What text box, **type *Fitzgerald* in the Replace With text box.**

d. **Click Find Next.**

e. **Click Replace.**

f. **Click Cancel** to close the Find And Replace dialog box.

g. **Close tblEmployees.** If prompted to save, **click No.**

h. **Close the SampleTables.mdb database.**

TOPIC F

Run a Report

You've used forms and queries to make working with table data easier and more efficient. You've even combined the skills to create an easy-to-use updating technique. Now it's time to add the finishing touch. In this topic, you will run a report that displays your data as a professionally formatted presentation.

You have been invited to a sales meeting and asked to distribute a listing of company products, organized by product line. This can be done by sorting the table or using different queries for each product line, but neither displays the data in a format you like. By running an Access report, you can produce a professionally formatted presentation you will be proud to distribute.

How to Run a Report

Procedure Reference: Run a Report

To run a report:

1. In the Database window, in the Objects pane, select Reports.

2. Run a report:

- Double-click the report you wish to run;
- Or, select the report you wish to run and press Enter.

3. Click Close to close the report.

ACTIVITY 2-6

Running a Report

Activity Time:

5 minutes

Data Files:

- UseReports.mdb

Scenario:

The consultant who set up your Access database created several reports and stored them in the UseReports.mdb database so you could get started. You will eventually need to create your own reports, and the consultant was kind enough to show you how to run the reports he created. By reviewing the tables that the reports pull data from, you can gain an understanding that will prepare you to create your own reports.

What You Do	How You Do It
1. In the UseReports.mdb database, **run the rptFinalReport report.**	a. **Open the UseReports.mdb database.**

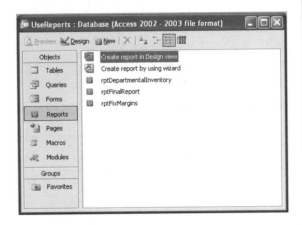

b. With Reports selected in the Objects pane, **double-click rptFinalReport** to run the report.

c. **Use the Zoom feature and size the report** so you can read it.

d. **Move though the report, then return to the top of the first page.**

---

2. **Was it necessary for any of the tables to be open for the report to run?**

---

3. **Record Rachel Middlebrook's asset tag, department number, and purchase price.**	a. In the Departmental Inventory report, **locate the entry for Rachel Middlebrook.**

b. From the entry, **record the following information:**

- Asset Tag: _____
- Department Number: _____
- Purchase Price: _____

c. **Close the report.**

---

4. Open tblComputers and locate the Asset Tag and purchase price you recorded.

    a. Open tblComputers.

    b. Locate the asset tag number you recorded.

    c. Locate the purchase price and compare it with the purchase price you recorded to verify that they match.

    d. Close tblComputers.

5. Verify that Rachel Middlebrook's department number in the report matches the one in the table.

    a. Open the tblEmployees table.

    b. Locate Rachel Middlebrook's record.

    c. Locate the department number and compare it with the number you recorded to verify that they are the same.

    d. Close tblEmployees.

    e. Close the database.

6. Did the information that appeared in the report come from a single table?

7. Why was it possible for the report to draw information from more than one table?

Lesson 2 Follow-up

In this lesson, you worked directly within an Access table to manage the table's data. You then used forms, queries, and reports to indirectly manage table data.

1. What types of operations can you perform on a table with an Access form?

2. How would you display a recordset?

LESSON 3

Establishing Table Relationships

Lesson Objectives:

In this lesson, you will examine existing table relationships.

You will:

- Examine tables with established relationships.
- Identify a table's primary and foreign keys.
- Examine and work with a table's Subdatasheets.

Introduction

As you have learned, the heart of any Access database is the table. Because Access is a relational database, it allows the data in different tables to be connected. This is a powerful concept that allows you to make use of the data in various tables, as if they were in a single table. In this lesson, you will learn how tables are connected and about an Access feature that allows you to create a quick summary of the data from the linked tables.

In a relational database, information you need often resides in several tables. Opening and searching for information in multiple tables can be time-consuming. However, Access allows tables to be connected and provides you with a feature that allows you to gather and summarize the information from the different tables in one convenient location.

TOPIC A

Identify Table Relationships

Using the form, query, and report objects, you have managed the records in a table. But working with the data in a single table only scratches the surface of the Access program. Because Access is a relational database, separate tables can be connected, allowing the user to make use of information in multiple tables. In this topic you will be introduced to tables with connections and launch a window with a visual display of the relationships.

Organizing complex data is the job of a relational database. For example, if your business has five product lines with 50 products in each line, organizing and displaying this in a single table could become overwhelmingly complex. By creating one table that holds information on the individual products, then connecting it to the appropriate product lines in a second table, you can manage any individual product in any product line in a simplified manner. Understanding how tables are connected and how to display the connections will allow you to make full use of the relational concept.

Table Relationships and the Relationships Window

Definition:

The purpose of relationships between tables is to link one set of information to another set of information.

Example:

The Access Relationships window is a graphic display of these relationships. The lines that connect the tables provide a visual indication of how the relationships work.

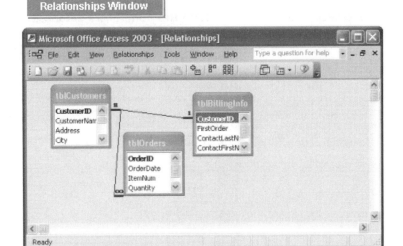

Figure 3-1: *The Relationships window.*

Analogy:

A highway system connecting Chicago, Dallas, New York, Los Angeles, San Francisco, and Miami allows people to travel between the cities. However, from your perspective the system is not visible. A satellite image displaying the highway connections would be similar to that of the Relationships window, displaying the links between the tables in a database.

ACTIVITY 3-1

Using the Relationships Window to Identify Table Relationships

Activity Time:

5 minutes

Data Files:

* Computers.mdb

Scenario:

If you could see a picture of how the tables are connected to one another it would help illustrate how a relational database works. By launching the Computers.mdb database and opening the Relationships window, a visual representation of the table connections will be displayed on your screen. This is just what you are looking for.

What You Do

How You Do It

1. Open the Computers database and the Relationships window.

   a. **Open the Computers database.**

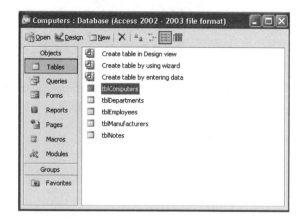

   b. On the toolbar, **click the Relationships button** to launch the Relationships window. This displays a graphic representation of the links between tables.

   c. If necessary, **maximize the window and resize the table displays** so all of the tables and connections in the display are visible.

2. According to the Relationships window, how many tables are connected in this database?

   a) One

   b) Three

   c) Five

   d) Seven

3. How many tables have more than one link to them?

   a) One

   b) Two

   c) Three

   d) Four

4. How many have more than two links?

   a) One

   b) Two

   c) Three

   d) Four

5. In the Relationships window, to which table(s) is the tblNotes table linked?

    a) tblComputers

    b) tblDepartments

    c) tblEmployees

    d) tblManufacturers

    e) tblNotes

TOPIC B

Identify Primary and Foreign Keys in the Relationships Window

You have launched the Relationships window and displayed the connections between the tables in your database. There are field names that are bold and different symbols displayed at the end points of the connecting lines. In this topic, you will examine the properties of the individual links that connect the tables.

Much of the power of a relational database is derived from the ability to connect information in different tables. The field is the point of connection. In order to establish the proper relationships, the connected fields have a differing status that is displayed in the Relationships window. In order to access the information in the linked tables, you must identify the status of the keys that make up the table connections.

Primary Keys

A *primary key* is a field or combination of fields containing a value that uniquely identifies a record. Primary keys are set in table Design view and identified by the small key icon to the left of the field name.

Primary Key Characteristics

The following list describes several characteristics and functions of primary keys:

- Primary keys are not required, but are strongly recommended in each table.
- Table relationships with referential integrity cannot be set without establishing primary keys.
- When creating subforms or subreports at the same time as a form or report, the Access wizards rely upon primary keys for form and report creation.

Foreign Keys

A *foreign key* is a field in one table that links to a primary key in another table.

How to Identify the Keys in Table Relationships

Procedure Reference: Identify Primary and Foreign Keys

To identify primary and foreign keys in the Relationships window:

1. Open the database.

2. On the toolbar, click the Relationships button.

3. Observe the links and keys. At a link's termination point (on either end), a bold field name represents a primary key, and a non-bold field name represents a foreign key.

ACTIVITY 3-2

Identifying the Keys in Table Relationships

Activity Time:

10 minutes

Setup:

The Computers.mdb database is open and the Relationships window is displayed.

Scenario:

You wish to learn more about the links between the tables, what they mean, and how to read them. To do so, you will review some examples and identify the different types of keys that comprise the links.

What You Do	How You Do It
1. Identify the Primary and Foreign keys in the Relationships window.	a. Examine the Relationships window and verify that there are links between all of the tables.

2. In tblDepartments, what type of key is DeptCode in the tblDepartments-tblEmployees relationship?

   a) Primary key

   b) Foreign key

   c) Primary and foreign key

3. In tblEmployees, what type of key is DeptCode in the tblDepartments-tblEmployees relationship?

   a) Primary key

   b) Foreign key

   c) Primary and foreign key

4. In the tblComputers-tblNotes relationship, in which table is AssetTag a primary key?

   a) tblComputers

   b) tblNotes

   c) Neither

   d) Both

   🖈 A Primary key can consist of multiple fields.

---

5. Close the Relationships window.   a. **Click Close.**

                                        b. If prompted, **do not save your changes.**

TOPIC C
Work with Subdatasheets

Understanding how tables are linked and what the purpose of the primary and foreign keys are in a table lets you identify and evaluate the possible relationships between tables. This helps you comprehend what is going on behind the scenes if you are working in a table and accessing the information in a table to which it is linked. In this topic, from an individual record in a table, you will launch a window that displays information from a linked table.

Understanding and knowing how Access tables are linked and evaluating the links between tables is a great starting point. But, if you are working in one table and you need to view the data in another linked table, how can you display it? The subdatasheet feature allows you to launch a window from any record that is linked to another table and display the data from the linked table.

Subdatasheets

Definition:

A subdatasheet is a datasheet that is nested within another datasheet and that contains data related or joined to the first datasheet. The subdatasheet is launched and the data in the joined table is displayed when the plus sign in the left column is clicked. The plus sign (+) in the first table is changed to a minus sign (–) when the subdatasheet is opened and then returns to a plus sign when the subdatasheet is closed.

Example:

In the following figure, the tblCustomers table is a datasheet that contains ID, name, and contact information for a company's customer base. By expanding the subdatasheet under one of the customer records, that customer's ordering history becomes visible.

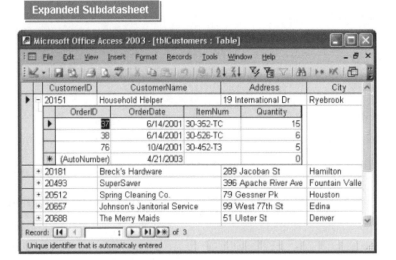

Figure 3-2: *A subdatasheet.*

How to Find Data in Subdatasheets

Procedure Reference: Find Data in Subdatasheets

To expand and collapse a subdatasheet:

1. Open the table you wish to use.

2. Locate the record you wish to view.

3. Click the plus sign (+) to the left of the record to expand the subdatasheet.

4. Click the minus sign (−) to the left of the record to collapse the subdatasheet.

5. Close the table.

ACTIVITY 3-3

Viewing Data in Subdatasheets

Activity Time:

5 minutes

Setup:

The Computers.mdb database is open.

Scenario:

You've been asked to locate purchase prices and warranty information on the company's computers. The only information you've been given are the employee's names. You thought there was a report, but there isn't. The information you need is contained in the tblEmployees tables.

What You Do	How You Do It
1. Open the tblComputers table and locate the purchase price of Lynne McMillan's computer, and then close the table.	a. Open the tblComputers table.
	b. **Attempt to locate Lynne McMillan's computer in the table.** While the information you need is in there, there is no way to identify it.
	c. Close tblComputers.

LESSON 3

2. **Open tblEmployees, locate Lynne McMillan, and record her Employee ID number.** Then, **expand her subdatasheet and record the purchase price of her computer.**

a. **Open tblEmployees.**

b. **Locate Lynne McMillan's record.**

c. From tblEmployees, **record her Employee ID:** _____.

d. In the column to the left, **click the plus sign and expand the subdatasheet.**

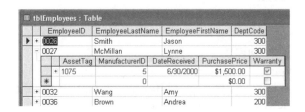

🔖 Notice that the plus sign turns to a minus sign indicating it is expanded.

e. **Record the computer's purchase price:** _____.

f. **Close the table without saving changes.**

3. If prompted, **open tblComputers and verify that the purchase price in the table matches the value in the subdatasheet.** Then, **close the table without saving.**

a. **Open tblComputers.**

b. **Locate Lynne McMillan's employee ID.**

🔖 You can use the Find button and search in the EmployeeID column.

c. **Verify that the value in the PurchasePrice field matches the value you recorded from the subdatasheet.**

🔖 The values displayed in the subdatasheet were extracted from the tblComputers table.

d. **Close tblComputers.** If prompted, **don't save changes.**

e. **Close the database.**

46   *Microsoft® Office Access 2003: Level 1*

4. Display the tblEmployees table and expand the subdatasheets for Eric Haygood and Norman Grakowsky.

a. Display the tblEmployees table.

b. In the tblEmployees table, **locate Eric Haygood's record.**

c. **Click the plus sign in the left column** to display the subdatasheet.

d. **Locate Norman Grakowsky's record.**

e. **Click the plus sign in the left column** to display the subdatasheet, and notice that all of the subdatasheets you've opened remain open.

f. **Close tblEmployees and the Computers database.**

Lesson 3 Follow-up

In this lesson, you launched the Relationships window and displayed and examined the links that connect the tables in an Access database.

1. **What window do you open to display the links between the tables in an Access database, and how are the links represented in the display?**

2. **What are the two types of keys that can be used to designate connections between linked tables?**

NOTES

LESSON 4

Querying the Database

Lesson Time
1 hour(s), 15 minutes

Lesson Objectives:

In this lesson, you will query the database.

You will:

*   Use the Access Query Wizard to create and name a query.
*   Add selection criteria to the query using Design view.
*   Add a calculated field to an Access query.
*   Modify a query to perform a summary calculation on a record grouping.

Introduction

In a previous lesson, you were introduced to the tools used to manage table data. One of the tools was a query. A query is a question that searches a database for information matching a specific set of conditions that you define. Queries can be developed and customized to your needs, then saved in the database and used whenever needed. This lesson will expand your Access knowledge to include creating and customizing queries.

Extracting data is another one of the most common operations performed on a database. Opening a table and searching through it one record at a time is inefficient, not to mention tiring. There's also the potential of introducing errors into your results. By creating a query you will have a customized, stored tool that can be used to accurately retrieve database information that meets specified criteria, whenever you need it.

TOPIC A

Create a Select Query

There are several different types of queries. Some are quite restricted in what they can do and you may not have a use for them at this point in your Access career. However, the most commonly used query, and the one you have already seen, is the Select query. In this topic, you will identify the different ways in which Select queries can assist you in performing your daily database responsibilities. You will also use the Query Design Wizard to create a query.

If you are like most users, after you become comfortable with Access you will begin thinking about ways to improve your daily operations. Querying databases to locate and manage information is one of the most common tasks you perform. Having used existing queries, you have likely thought of ideas for new queries that would make your life easier. By using the Query Design Wizard, you can create those custom queries and bring your dreams to life.

The Query Design Environment

A *Select query* is an Access object that selects and displays data that meets user-defined criteria from a table. The query may be viewed in Datasheet or Design view. When in Design view, the query's structure, properties, and function may be modified.

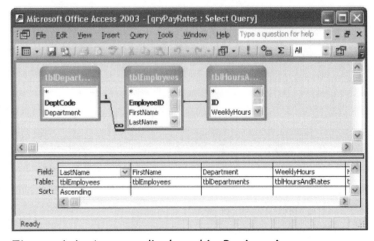

Figure 4-1: *A query displayed in Design view.*

The Query Design Buttons

The following table describes a few of the buttons on the Query Design toolbar.

Icon	Button Name	Description
	Query Type	Selects the query type.
	Run	Runs the query and displays the results.
	Show Table	Opens the Show Table dialog box.
Σ	Totals	Adds the Totals row to the query in Design view.
	Properties	Opens the query property sheet.
	Build	Launches the Expression Builder.

ACTIVITY 4-1

Examining the Select Query Type

Activity Time:

5 minutes

Data Files:

• SelectQueries.mdb

Scenario:

Your manager has asked you to find out which of the company's computers aren't covered by a warranty. You decide to use a Select query in order to quickly gather this information.

LESSON 4

What You Do	How You Do It
1. In the SelectQueries database, **open the qryNoWarranty query and examine the datasheet, and then switch to Design view.**	a. **Open the SelectQueries database.**

b. With Queries selected in the Objects pane, **double-click qryNoWarranty** to open the query.

c. **Examine the datasheet.** There are seven computers without warranties.

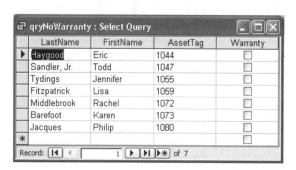

d. **Click the View button** to change to Design view.

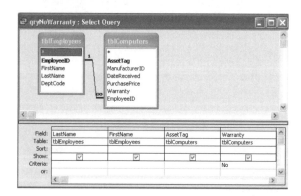

2. In the Warranty column, **change the criteria from No to Yes and run the query.**

   a. In the design grid, in the Criteria row of the Warranty field, **select No.**

   b. **Replace it with** *Yes*

   c. **Click the View button** to return to Datasheet view.

---

3. **How many records are now displayed?**

   a) 7

   b) 12

   c) 19

   d) 25

---

4. **Close the qryNoWarranty query window without saving changes to the design of the query.**

   a. **Click Close.**

   b. **Click No.**

How to Create a Select Query

Procedure Reference: Create a Select Query

To create a query using the wizard:

1. In the Database window, in the Objects pane, select Queries.

2. Double-click Create Query By Using Wizard.

3. Select the first table (or query) you wish to include in the query.

4. Add the fields you wish to include to the Selected Fields list.

5. Repeat steps 3 and 4 if you want to include any additional tables (or queries).

6. Click Next.

7. Select whether you want to view detail or summary information.

8. Click Next.

9. Name the query and select whether you want to open the query in Datasheet view or Design view.

10. Click Finish.

ACTIVITY 4-2

Creating a Select Query

Activity Time:

10 minutes

Setup:

The SelectQueries.mdb database is open.

Scenario:

You have been asked to produce a list of computers that includes the asset tag, manufacturer, date received, and purchase price. You will need data from fields in the tblComputers and tblManufacturers tables. By using the Query Wizard, you can create a query to locate and display the required data.

What You Do	How You Do It
1. **Launch the Query Wizard.**	a. With Queries selected in the Objects pane, **double-click Create Query By Using Wizard.**
2. Using tblComputers, **add the AssetTag, DateReceived, and PurchasePrice fields to the Selected Fields box.**	a. From the Tables/Queries drop-down list, **select Table: tblComputers.**

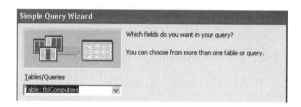

	b. **Click the right-pointing single arrow to** add the AssetTag field to the Selected Fields box.
	c. In the Available Fields list box, **select DateReceived.**
	d. **Click the right-pointing arrow.**

e. In the Available Fields list box, **double-click PurchasePrice.**

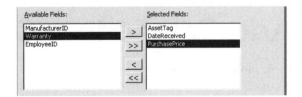

---

3. Using the tblManufacturers table, add the **Manufacturer** field to the query.

a. From the Tables/Queries drop-down list, **select Table: tblManufacturers.**

b. In the Available Fields list box, **double-click Manufacturer.**

c. **Click Next.**

---

4. **Verify that you want to see the detail records and continue.**

a. **Verify that Detail is selected, and then click Next.**

---

5. Give your query a title of *qryMyBrands*, complete the process and view the results of the query, and then examine the query in Design view.

a. In the title text box, **enter *qryMyBrands*** as the name of the query.

b. **Verify that Open The Query To View Information is selected and click Finish.**

c. In the toolbar, **click the View button** to change to Design view. The two tables are displayed and are joined on the ManufacturerID field. The fields you selected in the wizard are in the design grid.

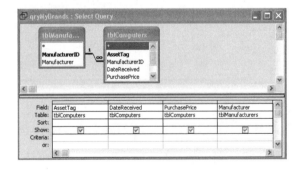

d. **Close the query.**

TOPIC B

Add Criteria to a Query

Even though you have now developed a Select query, the surface has just been scratched when it comes to querying. In this topic, you will look at the comparison operators and conditional operators that are used in Access queries to make them even more useful.

Let's say you have been asked to locate all of the records with an hourly rate of pay greater than $40 per hour, all of the records with work hours less than 30, and then a listing of the records for employees who work less than 30 hours and whose pay is greater than $40 per hour. You know the information is in the database and that a query is the tool you need to extract it, but how do you do it? By incorporating comparison operators and conditional operators into your query, you'll be able to access this information.

Comparison Operators

Including the comparison operators in an expression allows one data value to be compared against another, using a set of criteria that has been defined by the user. (An expression is a combination of symbols that produces a result. You'll learn more about them in the next topic.)

The Comparison Operators

The following table summarizes the comparison operators.

Operator	Value	Example
=	Equals	= 11/29/1961
<	Less than	< K
<=	Less than or equal to	<= 2500
>	Greater than	> K
>-	Greater than or equal to	>- 2500
<>	Not equal to	<> Michigan
Between And	Within a range	Between 5/1/2001 And 8/31/2001
Is Null	Null values	Is Null (just using "Null" will also work)

Conditional Operators

The AND, OR, and NOT conditional operators, also referred to as logical operators and Booleans, add the ability to evaluate the truth of an expression, thus increasing its flexibility and power.

The Conditional Operators

The following table summarizes the conditional operators.

Operator	Description	Example
AND	True if both conditions are true	> 5 AND <> 100
OR	True if either condition is true	< 5 OR > 500
NOT	True if the single instance is not true	NOT Between 100 And 200

Examples of Conditional Operators

The premise on which conditionals are based is that of truth. If the criteria in the expression are met, it is evaluated to be true. If the criteria is not met, it is evaluated to be false.

The Access query grid provides multiple rows in which one can identify what records are desired in the results. For example, if you wanted to select all the records where a price field is greater than $100, you could type >100 in the criteria row that is below the price field. Using ANDs and ORs would allow you to expand or narrow the search. If you want to select all the records where the price field is greater than $100 AND where the location of the sale is the state of California, you would add the word California to the criteria row below the State field. Both criteria should be placed on the same line. This automatically creates an AND condition. An AND condition narrows the search, and the records that are selected must meet *all* the criteria in order to be returned.

Putting criteria on a different line creates an OR condition, which expands the search. Using the previous example, if you were to move the word California down one row and across from the word *or*, to the left of the grid area, the query would return all the records where the price field is greater than $100 as well as all records where the state field is equal to California. Some prices may well be less than $100—but if they are in California, they meet the criteria. Some sales may be in Michigan, but as long as they are over $100, they meet the criteria.

AND and OR criteria may also be typed directly in the same cell. For example, one could type *California or Michigan* in a state criteria row to return all records from either state. Typing *California and Michigan* in a state criteria row would return no records, because the value in the state field cannot be equal to both.

How to Add Selection Conditions to the Query

Procedure Reference: Add Selection Conditions to the Query

To add selection criteria:

1. In the design grid, include the field or fields for which you want to set criteria.

2. Enter the first criterion in the Criteria row for the field.

3. To create an AND or OR condition on a single field, include the appropriate word in the criteria.

4. To create an AND condition on more than one field, enter the other criteria in the same Criteria row.

5. To create an OR condition on more than one field, enter the other criteria in the Or row.

ACTIVITY 4-3

Adding Selection Conditions to the Query

Activity Time:
10 minutes

Setup:
The SelectQueries Database window is displayed.

Scenario:
Comparison operators and conditional operators allow you to perform powerful searches, but can be confusing. Practicing with the queries in the SelectQueries.mdb database and using comparison operators and conditionals to search for computers that meet specific price, department code, or manufacturer criteria, and even looking for Null or blank fields in records will familiarize you with the operation of these features.

What You Do	How You Do It
1. Run the qryInventory query.	a. Double-click qryInventory.
2. How many records are displayed? a) 11 b) 21 c) 23 d) 32	
3. In Design view, use the > comparison operator in the PurchasePrice field's Criteria row to determine which computers cost more than $2,000, and then run the query.	a. Click the Design view button. b. Scroll to the right to view the PurchasePrice field in the design grid. c. Click in the Criteria row for the PurchasePrice field. d. Type >2000 e. Click the Datasheet view button and note that six records satisfy the condition.

4. Remove the PurchasePrice criteria and set the DeptCode equal to *500*, choose to not display the DeptCode field in the query datasheet, and then run the query.

   🖈 You do not have to enter the equal sign = in the criteria, and you do not have to display the field you use to set a condition.

   a. **Switch to Design view.**

   b. In the PurchasePrice field, **delete the >2000 criteria.**

   c. **Click in the Criteria row for the DeptCode field.**

   d. **Type *500***

   e. In the Show row, **uncheck the box for the DeptCode field.**

   f. **Switch to Datasheet view and observe the data.**

5. Switch to Design view, and in the Manufacturer field's Criteria row enter *Atlas* to add Atlas to the criteria. Then, **return to Datasheet view.**

   a. **Switch to Design view.**

   b. **Click in the Criteria row for the Manufacturer field.**

   c. **Type *Atlas***

   d. **Switch to Datasheet view.**

   e. **Examine the results.** Only two records satisfy this condition. By entering two conditions on the same Criteria row in the design grid, you create an AND condition and records must satisfy both conditions to be displayed in the query datasheet.

6. Switch to Design view and delete the existing condition in the Criteria row of the Manufacturer field, click in the Or row of the Manufacturer field and enter the manufacturer name *Cyber*, and then switch to Datasheet view to run the query and examine the results.

   🖈 Remember that you can create AND and OR conditions for the same field by including those operators in the criteria. For example, if you wanted to know how many Atlas and Cyber computers you have, you can enter the criteria "Atlas or Cyber."

   a. **Switch to Design view.**

   b. In the Criteria row of the Manufacturer field, **delete the existing condition.**

   c. In the Manufacturer field, **click in the Or row.**

   d. **Type *Cyber***

   e. **Switch to Datasheet view** to run the query.

7. **How many records are displayed?**

    a) 5

    b) 10

    c) 15

    d) 20

All computers assigned to the Technical Services department are included, as well as records for Cyber computers assigned to any department.

---

8. **Use the Between operator to create the criteria to determine how many computers were acquired during the first quarter of 2001.**

   Access automatically enters pound signs (#) around date values.

    a. **Switch to Design view.**

    b. **Delete the Cyber and 500 criteria.**

    c. **Click in the Criteria row for the DateReceived field.**

    d. **Type** *Between 1/1/2001 And 3/30/2001*

    e. **Run the query and verify that six records are displayed.**

---

9. **Use the Null operator to create a criterion in the tblComputers table to locate records with a blank value and save the query as** *qryMyMissingValues*.

    a. **Switch to Design view.**

    b. In the upper pane, **right-click the tblDepartments table.**

    c. **Choose Remove Table.**

    d. **Remove the tblManufacturers table** from the query.

    e. In the DateReceived field, **delete the criteria.**

    f. In the Criteria row for the ManufacturerID field, **type** *Is Null*

    g. **Run the query** and note that there are three records.

    h. **Save the query as** *qryMyMissingValues* **and click OK.**

    i. **Close the query window.**

TOPIC C

Add a Calculated Field to a Query

The ability to use Access comparison operators and conditional operators has greatly expanded your querying capacity. Now let's start using the values in a record to produce a result that is not in the record. In this topic, you will use arithmetic operators to create a query to perform a calculation on a value in a record and then display the results of the calculation in the query's output.

Managing money is an important function in all businesses, and for that matter, in your day-to-day life. Imagine that your company's payroll department wants you to calculate the weekly salary for an individual who is paid by the hour. By including a calculated field that uses the employee's hourly rate, this is easily accomplished.

Arithmetic Operators

Arithmetic operators are used to perform operations on table data. The arithmetic operators used in Access are the same operators used by other programs and applications, and they behave in a similar manner.

The Arithmetic Operators

The following table summarizes the arithmetic operators.

Operator	Description	Example	Result
+	Addition	value1 + value2	Value1 is added to value2
-	Subtraction	value1 - value2	Value2 is subtracted from value1
*	Multiplication	value1 * value2	Value1 is multiplied by value2
/	Division	value1 / value2	Value1 is divided by value2

Access Expressions

Simply put, Access *expressions* are combinations of identifiers, operators, and values that produce a result. Arithmetic expressions are composed of table data and the arithmetic operators + - * / . An expression may be simple or complex, but it usually results in a single value. The calculations are performed in a specific order, with the order of evaluation taking place from left to right. Precedence is dictated by the operators, in the following order:

1. Multiplication
2. Division
3. Addition
4. Subtraction

If a portion of the expression is enclosed in parentheses, that portion is evaluated first. If there are nested sets of parentheses, the innermost set is evaluated first.

ACTIVITY 4-4

Calculating Arithmetic Expressions

Activity Time:

5 minutes

Scenario:

You have been asked to incorporate several calculations in your query. Practicing with order of operation in expressions will help you accurately incorporate the calculations.

What You Do	How You Do It

1. **What is the answer to: 4 + (3 * 5)?**

    a) 12

    b) 14

    c) 17

    d) 19

    e) 35

2. **What is the answer to: (4 + 3) * 5?**

    a) 35

    b) 12

    c) 19

    d) 17

    e) 60

The Expression Builder

The Expression Builder is a tool that allows the user to select database objects and then, using the application's built-in operators and functions, build formulas and calculations that are used with queries and reports.

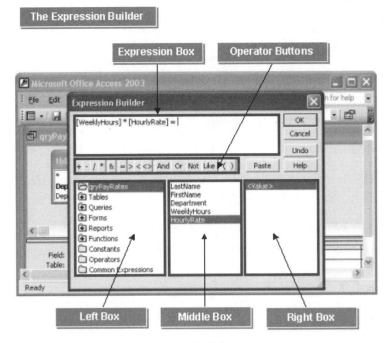

Figure 4-2: *The Expression Builder.*

The following table describes the components that comprise the Expression Builder.

Component	Function
Expression box	The location where the expression is built.
Operator buttons	The location where the operators used in the expression are selected.
Left box	Displays the table, query, form, report object, user-defined function, and other folders.
Middle box	If a left box folder is opened, the middle box will display the elements within that folder.
Right box	If a left box folder is opened and a category in the middle box is selected, the right box will display its related elements.

How to Add a Calculated Field to the Query

Procedure Reference: Add a Calculated Field to a Query

To add an arithmetic calculation:

1. In the query design grid, right-click in the first available blank column.

2. Choose Build.

3. Using the operator buttons and the lists of fields and functions, select and paste each component of the expression.

4. Click OK to enter the expression in the design grid.

ACTIVITY 4-5

Adding a Calculated Field to the Query

Activity Time:

10 minutes

Setup:

The SelectQueries database is open.

Scenario:

You have been asked to modify the qryPayRates query so that it calculates the weekly gross pay for all employees. By adding a calculated field, you can accomplish this task.

What You Do	How You Do It
1. Open the qryPayRates query in Design view and run the query.	a. Right-click the qryPayRates query.
	b. From the shortcut menu, **choose Design View.**
	c. **Observe the design.** It includes a tblHoursAndRates table and will display a list of employees and their hours and rates.
	d. **Switch to Datasheet view** to run the query.
2. Switch to Design view, right-click in the first blank column in the design grid and use the Expression Builder to create an arithmetic expression that multiplies weekly hours by the rate of pay, and then run the query and check the calculation.	a. **Switch to Design view.**
	b. In the design grid, **right-click in the first blank column to the right and choose Build** to open the Expression Builder.
	c. In the Expression Builder operator bar, **click the equal sign (=).**
	d. In the field list (the middle column), **double-click WeeklyHours.** Notice that the field name is added to the expression and is enclosed in brackets.
	e. In the operator bar, **click the multiplication sign (*).**

f. In the field list, **double-click HourlyRate.**

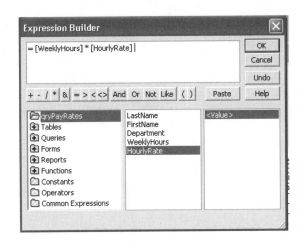

g. **Click OK** to close the Expression Builder.

h. **Run the query.**

3. **What is Rob Abbott's weekly pay?**

   a) 56

   b) 250

   c) 760

   d) 2,500

   Notice that the calculated field has a column heading of Expr1 and the values have a general number format.

4. **Open the Zoom dialog box, change the name of the calculated field to** *WeeklyGross*, **and then run the query.**

   a. **Switch to Design view.**

   b. **Right-click the calculated field and choose Zoom.**

   c. **Select Expr1 and type** *WeeklyGross*

   d. **Click OK** to close the Zoom dialog box.

e. **Run the query** to verify that WeeklyGross is displayed as the column heading.

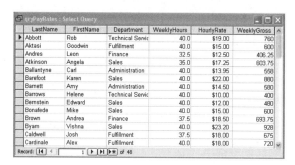

5. **Switch to Design view, open the Field Properties dialog box for the WeeklyGross field and set the Format property to Currency, and then run the query.**

   a. **Switch to Design view.**

   b. **Right-click the WeeklyGross field and choose Properties.**

   c. **Click in the Format property box.**

   d. From the drop-down list, **select Currency.**

   e. **Click the Close button** to close the Field Properties dialog box.

   f. **Run the query** and observe that the calculated values are displayed in currency format.

6. **Save the query as** *qryMyWeeklyGross*, **and then close it.**

   a. **Save the query as** *qryMyWeeklyGross*

   b. **Click OK.**

   c. **Close the select query.**

TOPIC D

Perform a Calculation on a Record Grouping

You now know how to use a query to perform a calculation on a single record. It is also important that you know how to perform a calculation based on a grouping of related records. In this topic, you will develop a query that selects a group of records and performs a calculation using all of the values in one of the group's fields.

One common, on-the-job use for Access is calculating payrolls by department. Developing a query that groups employees by department and then performs a payroll calculation on the departmental grouping will provide the results you need, and as a bonus, you can save the query and run it whenever necessary.

How to Perform a Calculation on a Group of Records

Procedure Reference: Perform a Calculation on a Record Grouping

To perform a calculation on a group of records:

1. To the design grid, add the field(s) on which you want to group records and the field(s) you wish to summarize.

2. Click the Totals button to display the Total row.

3. Enter any criteria necessary to select the records you wish to view.

4. If you need to enter criteria for a field on which you are not grouping records, include that field in the design grid and, from the Total drop-down list, select Where.

5. For each field, from the Total drop-down list, select Group By or the summary function.

6. Run the query.

LESSON 4

ACTIVITY 4-6

Performing a Calculation on a Group of Records

Activity Time:

10 minutes

Setup:

SelectQueries.mdb is open.

Scenario:

You have been asked by your manager to use the qryWeeklyInfo query to provide the average weekly hours for employees in each department and the total weekly gross payroll for each department.

What You Do	How You Do It
1. Run the qryWeeklyInfo query.	a. Run the qryWeeklyInfo query.
2. Switch to Design view and, on the toolbar, click the Totals button to add the Total row to the design grid.	a. Switch to Design view. b. Click the Totals button Σ. c. Examine the Total row that has been added to the grid.
3. Remove the LastName and FirstName columns from the design grid.	a. In the design grid, place the mouse pointer over the selector for the LastName column until it becomes a downward-pointing arrow and click to select the column. b. Press Delete. c. Select and delete the FirstName column.
4. In the Total row for the WeeklyHours field, enter the appropriate summary function to calculate the average weekly hours for each department.	a. Click in the Total row for the WeeklyHours field. b. From the drop-down list, select Avg.

5. In the Total row for the WeeklyGross field, enter the summary function to calculate the total weekly payroll for each department.

    a. Click in the Total row for the **WeeklyGross field.**

    b. From the drop-down list, **select Sum.**

    c. **Run the query.**

    d. **Compare your results to the following graphic.**

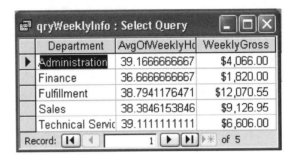

6. Switch to Design view and modify the format of the WeeklyHours field to display the average with one decimal place.

    a. If necessary, **size the columns so you can see the full column headings.**

    b. **Switch to Design view.**

    c. **Right-click the WeeklyHours field and choose Properties.**

    d. **Click in the Format property box.**

    e. From the drop-down list, **select Fixed.**

    f. From the Decimal Places drop-down list, **select 1.**

    g. **Close the Field Properties dialog box.**

7. Run the query, save the query as *qryMyTotals* and close the datasheet window, and then close the database window.

    a. **Run the query.**

    b. **Save the file as *qryMyTotals* and close the datasheet.**

    c. **Close the database.**

Lesson 4 Follow-up

In this lesson, you created a query. Working in a query's Design view, you also customized queries by adding comparison and conditional operators. You then used the Expression Builder to add a calculation to a field. Finally, you performed a calculation on a record grouping.

1. What are the two views used with a query, and which view can be used to modify the query?

2. What are the three types of operators used to build query expressions, and how are they used?

LESSON 5
Designing Forms

Lesson Objectives:

In this lesson, you will design simple forms.

You will:

- Discuss the form design overview.
- Create a form with the AutoForms feature.
- Create a form with a hidden object using the wizard.
- Select and modify objects on a form to change the design of the form.

Introduction

You have seen several different ways to manage data. On the job, you may be required to enter and update data on a regular basis. A custom form stored in your database that can be recalled each time you are required to perform these tasks can make life much simpler. In this lesson, you will create custom forms, and then modify the forms to meet your specific needs.

When opening a table in Datasheet view, the entire table, including all of the records and every field in each record, is displayed. In large tables with thousands of records, this can be overwhelming. Searching for individual records or fields can be time consuming, and the chance of making an error by misreading a value is increased. Creating a customized Access form that allows you to view and edit one record at a time will expedite the process and reduce errors.

TOPIC A

Examine Form Design Guidelines

You have used a form to enter and edit data in a table. Although an unlimited number of designs can be applied to a newly developed form, there are basic design principles that should be applied regardless of the use. Any easy-to-use form with an efficient design will be appreciated by all. In this topic, you will identify some of the design principles that should be applied to any form.

The form is one of the most often used data management tools. A well-designed form allows the user to view and enter data in a timely manner with a minimum of mistakes. Using the basic form design principles, you can develop forms that help ensure an efficient and error-free data entry process.

AutoForms

An AutoForm is a one-click form creation tool that automatically creates a form displaying every field in all records from the table or query on which it is based.

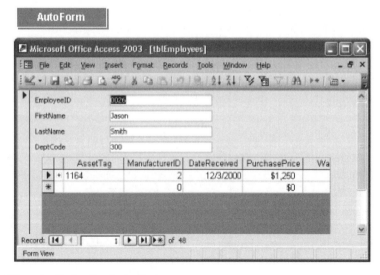

Figure 5-1: *An AutoForm.*

The AutoForm Feature

Creating forms from scratch is often time-consuming and unnecessary. While the results of the AutoForm aren't necessarily elegant, the user can usually modify the format of the form in less time than it would take to build it from scratch. The following list contains several features of the AutoForm:

- It can be used directly on a table or query using the New Object: AutoForm button.

- By default, the AutoForm button places all fields from the underlying table or query on the form.

- When launched with the New Object: AutoForm button, the final form displays one record per page in what is called the columnar layout.

- When working with multiple tables and/or when only specific fields need to be shown from a table, a query should be created first. The AutoForm button can be created from the query.

- The AutoForm option is also available from within the form object in the Database window by clicking the New button. This option allows the user to select from multiple layout options.

The Form Wizard

The Form Wizard is a useful tool for creating a more customized form. The Form Wizard:

- Uses guided questions to walk users through the form creation process.
- Can build a form based on more than one table.
- Offers design choices for both tabular and datasheet views.

Form Wizard Layouts

The four layouts available in the Form Wizard are summarized in the following table.

Form Layout	Features
Columnar	• One record appears per page. • Navigation buttons used to scroll through records. • Field placement easily modified. • Ability to modify field controls (e.g., fonts, colors, and background).
Tabular	• Multiple records appear per page. • Navigation typically done using the scroll bar. • Field placement can be modified and individual field controls can be formatted.
Datasheet	• Multiple records appear per page. • Looks and feels like a spreadsheet to the user. • Designer has minimal control over field placement and formatting.
Justified	• One record appears per page. • Navigation buttons used to scroll through records. • Field placement is stacked, starting horizontally and then moving vertically when they do not all fit within the form's width.

How to Identify the Form Design View

When opened in Design view, a form may consist of three general sections:

- The Header section is where information to be displayed at the top of the form is located.

- The Detail section is where the record data is contained.

- The Footer section is where the information to be displayed at the bottom of the form is located.

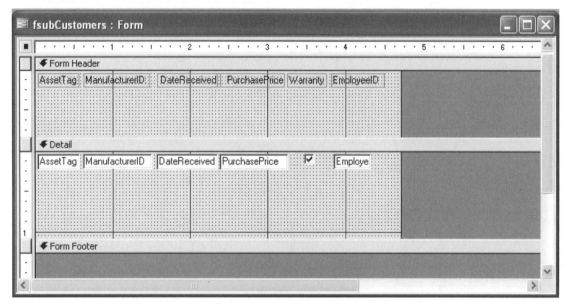

Figure 5-2: *A form displayed in Design view.*

ACTIVITY 5-1

Examining the Form Design Guidelines

Activity Time:

5 minutes

Scenario:

Reviewing some common-sense examples of the form design guidelines can assist you when you develop your first form.

What You Do	How You Do It

1. **When designing a form, who should you keep foremost in mind?**

   a) Your boss

   b) Your co-worker

   c) The user

   d) The consultant

2. In Design view, which section of a form would typically contain page numbering information?

    a) Header

    b) Detail

    c) Footer

3. Which of the Form Wizard layout styles shows multiple records per page?

    a) Columnar

    b) Tabular

    c) Datasheet

    d) Justified

TOPIC B

Create a Form Using AutoForm

Now that you have learned about some basic form design principles, imagine that you have been asked to immediately create a form to enter and edit data. Even knowing the design principles, developing the perfect form requires time, which you don't have. Luckily, the AutoForm tool will allow you to create a usable form in a minimum amount of time.

Even the most experienced form designers need time to plan and create custom forms. Until you have experience developing your own forms, it will take even longer. Perhaps there is an immediate need for the form, or the form will be used on a temporary basis and you don't wish to invest the time to plan and create the perfect form. By using the AutoForm feature, you can quickly create a basic default form that can be used with any designated table.

How to Create an AutoForm

Procedure Reference: Create an AutoForm

To create an AutoForm:

1. In the Database window, in the Objects pane, select Tables.

2. From the table list, select the table for which you want to create an AutoForm.

3. Click the NewObject: AutoForm button.

4. Save the form.

ACTIVITY 5-2

Creating a Form with the AutoForm Feature

Activity Time:

5 minutes

Data Files:

- UseForms.mdb

Scenario:

A co-worker has asked if you can create a form to access data in the UseForms database's tblCustomers and tblEmployees tables. By using the AutoForms Wizard, you can produce forms for both tables.

What You Do	How You Do It
1. Open the tblCustomers table.	a. With the UseForms database open, **open the tblCustomers table.**
2. Create an AutoForm based on the tblCustomers table.	a. On the toolbar, **click the New Object: AutoForm button** 🔲 ▾ .
3. _____ True or False? The number of fields in the form is the same as the number of fields in the table.	
4. _____ True or False? New records can be added to the table with the AutoForm you created.	
5. Close the form and save it as *frmMyCustomers*.	a. **Click the Close button** to close the tblCustomers form.
	b. **Click Yes.**
	c. Type *frmMyCustomers*
	d. **Click OK.**
	e. **Close tblCustomers.**
6. Create an AutoForm based on the tblEmployees table, with a link to another table that includes a subdatasheet display.	a. From the list of tables in the UseForms Database window, **select tblEmployees.**
	b. From the toolbar, **click the New Object: AutoForm button.**

c. **Examine the form.**

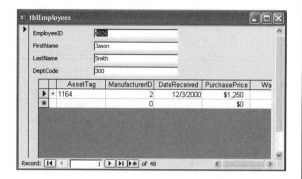

 This is a combination of a form and a subform. The relationship between the two is similar to the relationship between the datasheet and subdatasheet that was discussed earlier in the course.

7. _____ **True or False? The subdatasheet will expand if you click the plus sign (+) in the form.**

8. **Expand the subdatasheet, and then close the subdatasheet.**

   a. **In the first record displayed in the AutoForm, click the expand indicator (+)** and notice that related data from a third table is displayed.

   b. **Click the collapse indicator (-).**

9. **Use the mouse pointer to widen the form window, and then attempt to widen the datasheet to view the entire record.**

   a. **Place the mouse pointer over the right side of the form window until it becomes a horizontal double-headed arrow.**

   b. **Click and drag the right edge of the form window to the right.**

   c. **Place the mouse pointer over the right edge of the datasheet.** The horizontal sizing pointer is not displayed; the size of the datasheet must be adjusted in the form's Design view.

       Column widths in the datasheet can be adjusted by dragging the right edge of the column heading.

10. **Save and close the form.**

    a. **Save the form as *frmMyEmployees* and close the form.**

    b. **Close any open tables.**

TOPIC C

Create a Form Using the Form Wizard

The AutoForm feature, which is actually an Access wizard, is limited in the design of the forms it produces. The true power of using a form is derived from an interface that presents data in an easily understood format and provides the user with a virtually error-proof data entry capability.

As the person in your business who has received training in Access, you may be looked upon as the resident Access expert and called upon to create custom forms for the users. With the Access Form Wizard you will be able to accommodate the requests and develop forms that display only the information needed, in an easy-to-understand format that reduces data entry errors.

How to Create a Form with the Form Wizard

Procedure Reference: Create a Form with the Form Wizard

To create a form with the wizard:

1. In the Database window, in the Objects pane, select Forms.

2. Double-click Create Form By Using Wizard.

3. From the Tables/Queries drop-down list, select the first data source for the form.

4. Add the fields you want in the form to the Selected Fields list.

5. Repeat Steps 3 and 4 for any additional data sources and fields. Click Next.

6. If you have fields from more than one table, decide how you want the wizard to organize them. Then decide whether you want subforms or linked forms for the related data. Click Next.

7. Choose the form layout and click Next.

8. Choose the form style and click Next.

9. Enter a title for the form and, if necessary, the subform. Select the view in which you want to open the form.

10. Click Finish.

11. Close the form.

Activity 5-3

Creating a Form with the Form Wizard

Activity Time:

10 minutes

Setup:

The UseForms database is open.

Scenario:

This time, your manager has asked you to create a more complex form that displays all of the fields from the tblEmployees table and the AssetTag, DateReceived, PurchasePrice, and Warranty fields from the tblComputers table of the UseForms database. He would also like a particular layout applied to the finished product. The Form Wizard will allow you to complete this task.

What You Do	How You Do It
1. **Start the Form Wizard.**	a. In the Objects pane, **select Forms.**
	b. **Double-click Create Form By Using Wizard.**
2. **Add all the tblEmployees fields to the form, and then,** from the tblComputers table, **add the AssetTag, DateReceived, PurchasePrice, and Warranty fields.**	a. From the Tables/Queries drop-down list, **select Table: tblEmployees.**
	b. **Click the right-pointing double arrow** to add all the fields in the table to the Selected Fields list.
	c. From the Tables/Queries drop-down list, **select Table: tblComputers.**
	d. In the Available Fields list, **verify that AssetTag is selected.**
	e. **Click the right-pointing single arrow.**
	f. In the Available Fields list, **select DateReceived.**
	g. **Click the right-pointing single arrow.**

h. **Add the PurchasePrice and Warranty fields to the Selected Fields list.**

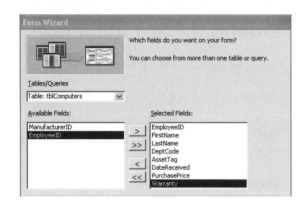

i. **Click Next.**

3. **Preview the form, decide whether you want a form with subforms or linked forms, and select the option that enables you to open only one form. Continue to the next page of the wizard.**

a. **Observe the preview of the form.** The view is by tblEmployees.

b. **Select by tblComputers** and observe the preview.

c. **Select by tblEmployees.**

d. **Verify that Form With Subform(s) is selected** and observe the preview.

e. **Select Linked Forms** and observe the preview.

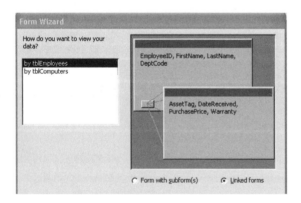

f. **Select Form With Subform(s).**

g. **Click Next.**

4. Observe the Datasheet layout, and then select Tabular. Continue to the next page of the wizard.	a. Observe the preview for the Datasheet layout.
	b. Select Tabular and observe the preview.
	c. Click Next.
5. Observe the available styles and select a style. Continue to the next page of the wizard.	a. In the list of styles, select each style and observe the preview.
	b. Select the style you prefer.
	c. Click Next.
6. Give the form a title of *frmMyEmployees2*, give the subform a title of *sbfMyComputersSubform*, and then open the form.	a. In the Form text box, type *frmMyEmployees2*
	b. In the Subform text box, type *sbfMyComputersSubform*
	c. Verify that Open The Form To View Or Enter Information is selected.
	d. Click Finish and examine the form.
7. Close the form.	a. Click Close.

TOPIC D

Modify the Design of a Form

As with any creation, there are generally improvements that can be made. Imagine that you have been asked by users to alter the order and alignment of some of the form's controls, and change the title of some of the labels. In this topic, you will modify the size, alignment, positions, and labels of the controls on your form.

The form you created with the wizard is perfectly usable and fulfills its intended function. But, after using the form for a while, you've identified some possible changes in the design and several users have also offered helpful suggestions. A custom form can be seen as a living object; by modifying the design of your form it will become even more efficient and error-proof, and you will continue to enhance your reputation as the corporate Access expert.

Controls

Definition:

A *control* is an object that allows the user to control the program. Controls are used to display data, allow user input, or perform an action. Controls are commonly used on forms and reports. Controls can be selected, sized, aligned, and moved to present a professional appearance. They generally are labeled with context-significant names so that their purpose is easily identified by the user.

Example:

Some examples of controls include text boxes, labels, rectangles, combo boxes, lines, and graphics.

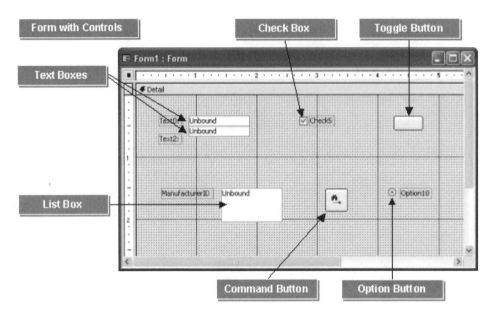

Figure 5-3: *Examples of controls.*

Selecting Form Controls

To modify a form's controls, they must first be selected. There are four methods of selecting controls:

- Click to select a single control.
- Select contiguous controls with the lasso technique.
- Use the appropriate ruler to select all of the controls in a horizontal or vertical line.
- Use the Shift-click technique to select non-contiguous controls.

ACTIVITY 5-4

Selecting Controls

Activity Time:

5 minutes

Setup:

The UseForms.mdb database is open.

Scenario:

Your manager wants you to customize your form. First you need to learn how to work in the form design environment. When you open a form in Design view, you realize that you need practice selecting the controls that are on the form. Using the different selection techniques to select controls on the frmSelectControls form will prepare you to move controls on other forms.

What You Do	How You Do It
1. Open the frmSelectControls form in Design view and select the text box control holding the CustomerName field, and then select the label control for the field.	a. **Open the frmSelectControls form in Design view.**
	b. **Click the text box containing the CustomerName field.** Note that the control has selection handles on all sides.
	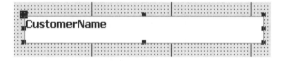
	c. **Click the label control for the CustomerName field.** The label control has selection handles and the text box has only a move handle.
	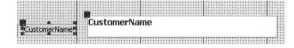
2. Use the lasso technique to select controls and observe the selection handles, and then deselect the controls.	a. **Position the mouse pointer above and to the left of the CustomerName label.**

b. **Click and drag to draw a rectangle that touches the CustomerName label in the upper-left and the Fax text box in the lower-right.** Note that all the controls have selection handles.

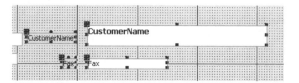

c. **Click a blank portion of the form** to deselect the controls.

3. **Use the click-in-ruler technique to select the labels and text boxes, observe the selection handles, and then deselect the controls.**

a. **Click the vertical ruler at the 1.75-inch mark** and observe the selection handles.

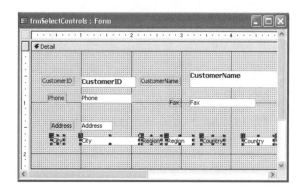

b. **Click a blank portion of the form** to deselect the controls.

4. Using the ruler to select the labels and text boxes, observe the selection handles and deselect the controls.

   a. Click at the 0.5-inch mark on the horizontal ruler.

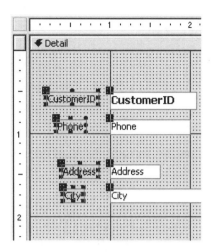

   b. Click and drag the 0.5-inch mark on the horizontal ruler to about the 1.5-inch mark and observe the selection handles.

   c. Deselect the controls.

5. Using the Shift-click technique to select controls, observe the selection handles and deselect the controls.

   a. Click the CustomerID text box.

   b. Press and hold the Shift key, and then click both the Fax text box and the PostalCode text box.

   c. Release the Shift key.

   d. Click a blank area to deselect the controls.

Sizing Form Controls

Sizing controls to be proportionate to their use is a critical design component. There are three methods of sizing controls:

- Drag a sizing handle to increase or decrease the size.

- From the menu, choose Format→Size→To Fit.

- Select multiple controls, choose Format→Size, and choose whichever option is appropriate.

> The same options available from the Format menu are available by right-clicking a selected control and choosing Size from the shortcut menu.

ACTIVITY 5-5

Sizing Controls

Activity Time:

5 minutes

Setup:

The frmSelectControls form of the UseForms database is open in Design view.

Scenario:

You've found that when you create an AutoForm or a form with the wizard, the controls are not always the right size. Sometimes they're bigger than you need or they occupy extra space on the form. Other times, they're not big enough and you can't view all of the data from a field. You want to make them the correct size.

What You Do	How You Do It
1. View the data in three records.	a. Switch to Form view.
	b. On the navigation bar, **click the Next Record button three times.**
2. Which text box controls appear to be too small?	

    a) Address text box

    b) Postal Code label

    c) Postal Code text box

    d) Region label

3. In Design view, **resize the CustomerID and the Address text boxes.**

   a. In Design view, **click the CustomerID text box.**

   b. **Place the mouse pointer over the sizing handle in the middle of the right side of the text box until it becomes a horizontal double-headed arrow and click and drag the sizing handle to the left until the text box is 0.5 inches wide.** View and use the horizontal ruler to judge the width.

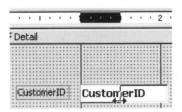

   c. **Click the Address text box.**

   d. Using the middle sizing handle on the right side, **click and drag to make the text box about 2 inches wide.**

4. **Size the PostalCode text box to fit its contents.**

   a. **Click the PostalCode text box.**

   b. **Choose Format→Size→To Fit.**

5. **Make the CustomerID text box the height of the CustomerName text box, and then undo the sizing.**

   a. **Click the CustomerID text box.**

   b. **Press and hold the Shift key and click the Customer Name text box.**

   c. **Choose Format→Size→To Tallest.**

   d. **Click the Undo button.**

6. **Make the Fax text box the same size as the Phone text box.**

   a. **Select the Fax and Phone text boxes.**

   b. **Right-click one of the selected text boxes.**

   c. **Choose Size→To Narrowest.**

7. Save the form as *frmMyControls*, and then view the form.

   a. Choose File→Save As.

   b. Save the form as *frmMyControls*

   c. View the form.

Aligning and Spacing Form Controls

Aligning controls and adjusting the spacing between them improves the appearance of a form or report. To do this:

- Select the controls you want to align and right-click one of them. From the shortcut menu, choose Align. You can then choose to align the Left, Right, Top, or Bottom sides, or to align To Grid.

- To even out horizontal or vertical spacing of controls, select the controls and choose either Format→Horizontal Spacing or Format→Vertical Spacing. You can choose to adjust the spacing by selecting Make Equal, Increase, or Decrease.

ACTIVITY 5-6

Aligning and Spacing Controls

Activity Time:

5 minutes

Setup:

The frmSelectControls form of the UseForms database is displayed.

Scenario:

The format of frmSelectControls looks better, but the alignment still needs some work. By using alignment techniques you can improve the appearance.

What You Do	How You Do It
1. With frmSelectControls open in Design view, **align the right side label controls.**	a. In Design view, **click the horizontal ruler to select the CustomerID, Phone, Address, and City label controls.**
	b. **Right-click one of the selected controls and choose Align→Right.**

2. Align the Phone and Fax labels and text boxes so the bottoms of the controls are even.

    a. Use the vertical ruler or the lasso technique to select the Phone and Fax labels and text boxes.

    b. Right-click a selected control and choose Align→Bottom.

3. Make the spacing of the City, Region, Country, and PostalCode labels and text boxes equal.

    a. Select the City, Region, Country, and PostalCode labels and text boxes.

    b. Choose Format→Horizontal Spacing→ Make Equal.

4. View and then save and close the form.

    a. View the form.

    b. Save and close the form.

Moving Form Controls

In order to move a control, you need to watch for the correct mouse pointer to be displayed. This change in the mouse pointer will occur as you point to the move handle of the control you want to move. There are two conditions for moving controls:

- If you want to move just the text box or label, and not its associated component, the mouse pointer should look like a hand with a single pointing finger 🖐 .

- If you want to move the text box or label and its associated component, or a grouping of controls, the mouse pointer should look like a hand with all of the fingers extended 🖐 .

ACTIVITY 5-7

Moving Controls

Activity Time:

10 minutes

Setup:

The UseForms database is open.

Scenario:

A few final movements of some of the controls will improve your form. You are now in the area where a lot of the improvements are a matter of taste, so getting some feedback from users is a good idea.

What You Do	How You Do It
1. Move the CustomerName text box closer to its label.	a. In the UseForms Database window, right-click frmMoveControls and choose Design View.
	b. Select the CustomerName text box.
	c. Place the mouse pointer over the move handle in the upper-left corner of the text box until it becomes a hand with a pointing finger.
	d. Click and drag the text box to the left to place it closer to the CustomerName label.
2. Move the CustomerID label and text box to the upper-left corner of the form.	a. Click the CustomerID text box.
	b. Place the mouse pointer over the top or bottom edge of the text box until it becomes an open hand.
	c. Click and drag the label and the text box to the upper-left corner of the form.

3. Move the Fax label closer to the Fax text box.	a. Click the Fax label.
	b. Place the mouse pointer over the move handle in the upper-left corner of the label until it becomes a hand with a pointing finger.
	c. Click and drag it closer to the Fax text box.
4. Move all the labels and text boxes containing address information lower on the form.	a. Use the ruler or lasso technique to select all of the labels and text boxes containing address information.
	b. Place the mouse pointer over all of the selected controls until it becomes an open hand.
	c. Click and drag the controls down on the form.
5. Close the form without saving changes.	a. Click the Close button.
	b. Click No.

How to Modify a Form

Procedure Reference: Modify a Form

To modify a form:

1. Display the form in Design view.

2. Select the controls you wish to work with.

3. Move the controls.

   - If you want to move just the text box or label, and not its associated component, the mouse pointer should look like a hand with a single pointing finger.

   - If you want to move the text box or label and its associated component, or a grouping of controls, the mouse pointer should look like a hand with all of the fingers extended.

4. Size the controls.

   - Drag a sizing handle to increase or decrease the size.

   - From the menu, choose Format→Size→To Fit.

   - Select multiple controls, choose Format→Size, and choose whichever option is appropriate.

> ✏ The same options available from the Format menu are available by right-clicking a selected control and choosing Size from the shortcut menu.

5. Align the controls and adjust their spacing.

   - Select the controls you want to align and right-click one of them. From the shortcut menu, choose Align. You can then choose to align the Left, Right, Top, or Bottom sides, or to align To Grid.

   - To even out horizontal or vertical spacing of controls, select the controls and choose either Format→Horizontal Spacing or Format→Vertical Spacing. You can choose to adjust the spacing by selecting Make Equal, Increase, or Decrease.

6. If necessary, adjust the tab order of the form fields.
   a. In Design view, choose View→Tab Order.
   b. In the Tab Order dialog box, click Auto Order.
   c. Click OK.

7. Apply formatting to text boxes or labels.

8. Add a title or other descriptive text.

9. Change the size of the form.

10. Save your changes under an appropriate name.

ACTIVITY 5-8

Modifying a Form

Activity Time:

10 minutes

Setup:

The UseForms Database window is displayed.

Scenario:

Your manager has asked you to improve the appearance of a wizard-created form using the design techniques you have learned. By applying these techniques to the frmGSCCustomers form, you will turn it into a professional looking creation your organization will be proud of.

What You Do	How You Do It
1. Open the frmGSCCustomers form and size the form to the screen.	a. Right-click frmGSCCustomers and choose Design View.
	b. Place the mouse pointer over the lower-right corner of the form window until it becomes an angled double-headed arrow.
	c. Drag down and to the right to enlarge the window.
	d. Place the mouse pointer over the right edge of the form until it becomes a vertical line with a horizontal double-headed arrow.
	e. Click and drag the edge of the form to the 6-inch mark on the right of the ruler.
	f. Place the mouse pointer over the bottom edge of the form and drag the edge down to the 3-inch mark.
2. Using selection, moving, sizing, and alignment techniques, arrange the controls on the form so that it is similar to the graphic shown in Step 2d.	a. Move the CustomerName controls up next to the CustomerID controls.
	b. Move the Address controls down on the form so you have room to arrange the Phone and Fax controls.
	c. Size the Phone and Fax text boxes and move the labels closer to the text boxes.
	d. Align the controls so they are similar to the following graphic.

3. Switch to Form view and check the tab order.

    a. **Switch to Form view.**

    b. **Press the Tab key eight times** to move from the first field in the form to the last. The Phone field would logically follow the CustomerName field in the form's new layout, but the tab order is based on the original layout.

4. Return to Design view and correct the tab order.

    a. **Switch to Design view.**

    b. **Choose View→Tab Order.**

    c. In the Tab Order dialog box, **click Auto Order, and then click OK.**

5. Return to Form view and check the tab order.

    a. **View the form.**

    b. **Press the Tab key** to move through the fields. The tab order has been corrected to better suit the form's new layout.

6. Save the form as *frmMyGSCCustomers*, and then close the form.

    a. **Save the form as *frmMyGSCCustomers***

    b. **Close the form, then close the database.**

Lesson 5 Follow-up

In this lesson, you first created a simple AutoForm and then used the Form Wizard to create a custom form. You then selected, sized, aligned, and moved controls to modify the form to meet your specific needs.

1. **What is the primary difference between creating a form with the AutoForm feature and the Form Wizard?**

2. **What types of forms will you create to work with your data?**

LESSON 6
Producing Reports

Lesson Time
1 hour(s)

Lesson Objectives:

In this lesson, you will create and modify Access reports.

You will:

- Create a report with the AutoReport feature.
- Create a report with the wizard.
- Examine a report in Design view.
- Add a calculated field to the report.
- Modify the properties that set the appearance of a control.
- Modify the format of a report by using the AutoFormat feature.
- Adjust the width of a report.

Introduction

One of the most powerful management tools in a database is the report. On the job you will most likely be asked to produce reports on a regular basis. In this lesson, you will use the Access report development and design tools to create custom reports.

Compiling and analyzing data can allow a business to examine past trends and predict future directions. In large databases with many tables, each of which may contain thousands of records, gathering and reporting can be difficult and time consuming. Creating and using customized Access reports can provide you with an efficient tool that simplifies your reporting requirements and can be saved for future use.

TOPIC A

Create an AutoReport

Much like the AutoForm feature, AutoReport can be used to quickly create a simple report that contains all of the fields in a specific table. This topic will introduce you to the AutoReport feature and how to use it to quickly create a simple report.

Designing a complex report requires time and planning. You will no doubt encounter situations when there is not the time for either. Or, perhaps the report will only be used once and there is no need to create the perfect report. Using the AutoReport tool you can create a report that displays all of the fields for any given table.

AutoReport

The AutoReport feature allows the user to create a one-click report with a standardized format. It is almost instantaneous and often used when timeliness is a factor. The AutoReport feature:

- Launches with the toolbar's New Object: AutoReports button and works directly with a table or query.
- By default selects all the fields from the underlying table or query and places them on the report.
- Can make use of multiple tables.
- Is also available from within the Report Design Wizard for the three most common layout types (columnar, tabular, and justified).

How to Create an AutoReport

Procedure Reference: Create an AutoReport

To create an AutoReport:

1. In the Database window, select the table or query on which you want to base the report.

2. On the toolbar, from the New Object drop-down list, select AutoReport.

3. Save the report.

ACTIVITY 6-1

Creating a Report with the AutoReport Wizard

Activity Time:

10 minutes

Data Files:

*   UseReports.mdb

Scenario:

Before an urgent request for printed output of your data arises, you've decided to prepare for the situation and review the results of an AutoReport in Print Preview mode. This way, you'll know what to expect before you actually print a report.

What You Do	How You Do It
1. In the UseReports database, **run the qryInventory query and view the results in Print Preview format. Print the report.**	a. In the UseReports database, **double-click the qryInventory query.**
	b. **Click the Print Preview button.**
	c. **Enlarge the preview to 100%.**
	d. **Using the scroll and navigation bars, modify the display as necessary to view both pages.**

 The ability to print will depend upon your classroom setup. Your instructor will advise you on this.

e. From the menu, **choose File→Print and click OK** to send the output to the printer.

f. **Examine the printed output.**

2. **What features does the printed datasheet have?**

3. **What disadvantages are there to printing the query datasheet?**

4. **Create an AutoReport.**

    a. **Close Print Preview.** If necessary, reopen qryInventory in Datasheet view.

    b. From the New Object: AutoForm drop-down list, **choose AutoReport.**

---

5. **Examine the preview of the AutoReport.**

    How does the AutoReport compare to the printed datasheet?

---

6. **Close the preview window and save the report as *rptMyAutoReport*. If necessary, close the report Design window.**

    a. **Close the preview window.**

    b. When prompted to save, **click Yes.**

    c. In the Report Name text box, **type *rptMyAutoReport***

    d. **Click OK.**

    e. If necessary, **close the report Design window.**

    f. If necessary, **close the qryInventory query.**

Topic B

Create a Report by Using the Wizard

Like AutoForms, the AutoReport feature is a wizard, also limited in the scope of the reports it produces. Similar to using forms, the real advantages gained from reports lies in the custom report. The custom report can provide the business with a tool to evaluate past and present activities and to plan for the future. By using the Report Wizard, you can create custom reports to begin to realize the advantages of database reporting.

At your business, you may be called upon to create custom reports. With the Report Wizard, you will be able to develop reports that display the information requested.

The Report Wizard

The Report Wizard is the recommended method for creating reports. The Report Wizard has the following features:

*   It walks users through the report creation process with guided questions.

- It will build a report based on more than one table.
- It offers design choices, including the columnar, tabular, and justified views.

How to Create a Report with Wizard

Procedure Reference: Create a Report with the Wizard

To create a report with the wizard:

1. In the Database window, in the Objects pane, select Reports.

2. Double-click Create Report By Using Wizard.

3. From the Tables/Queries drop-down list, select the data source for the report.

4. Move the fields you want included in the report from the Available Fields list to the Selected Fields list by using the arrow buttons.

5. Repeat Steps 3 and 4 for any additional data sources.

6. Click Next.

7. If necessary, choose the grouping levels and grouping options you want, and click Next.

8. Select the sort order for the detail records and click Next.

9. Select the layout for the report and click Next.

10. Select the style for the report and click Next.

11. Enter a title for the report and select whether you want the report displayed in Print Preview or Design view.

12. Click Finish.

ACTIVITY 6-2

Creating a Report with the Report Wizard

Activity Time:

15 minutes

Setup:

The UseReports.mdb database is open.

Scenario:

The Controller of your organization has asked for a report that lists, by department, the current computer inventory. You want to organize the information correctly and print it in a legible, professional-looking format. The Report Wizard will create a report that accomplishes this.

LESSON 6

What You Do	How You Do It
1. **Start the Report Wizard.**	a. In the Database window, **display Reports.**
	b. **Double-click Create Report By Using Wizard.**

2. From Query: qryInventory, **select the fields with which you will be working.**

a. With Query: qryInventory selected in the Tables/Queries drop-down list, **click the right-pointing double arrow** to move all the available fields to the Selected Fields list.

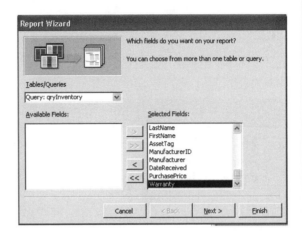

b. In the Selected Fields list, **select ManufacturerID.**

c. **Click the left-pointing single arrow.**

d. **Remove the Warranty field from the Selected Fields list.**

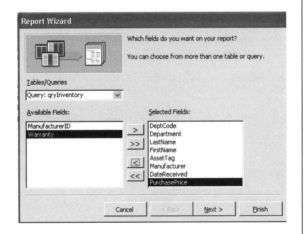

e. **Click Next.**

3. **View some examples of the available views and groupings. Then click Show Me More Information.**

   a. In the list of views, **click By tblEmployees and view the sample.**

   b. In the list of views, **click By tblComputers and view the sample.**

   c. In the list of views, **click By tblManufacturers and view the sample.**

   d. **Click Show Me More Information** to display the Report Wizard Tips.

---

4. **Close the Report Wizard Tips, and then choose tblDepartments and continue through the wizard.**

   a. In the Report Wizard Tips dialog box, **click Close.**

   b. If necessary, in the list of views, **select tblDepartments.**

   c. **Click Next.**

   d. Since you don't need any additional levels of groups, **click Next.**

---

5. **Sort the detail records in ascending order, by asset tag number.**

   a. From the drop-down list for the first sort box, **select AssetTag.**

   b. **Click Next.**

---

6. **View the layout samples and apply the Outline 1 layout.**

   a. In the Layout section, **select each option and view the sample.**

   b. **Select Outline 1.**

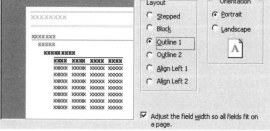

   c. **Click Next.**

---

7. **View the style samples and apply the Corporate style.**

   a. In the list of styles, **select each style and view the sample.**

b.   **Select Corporate.**

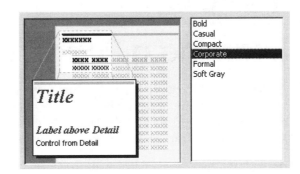

c.   **Click Next.**

---

8.   **Enter a title of *rptMyDepartments* and preview your report.**

     🖋 When previewing a report, you can use the Two Pages and Multiple Pages buttons to get a big-picture look at the layout of your report.

a.   In the title text box, **type *rptMyDepartments***

b.   **Verify that Preview The Report is selected.**

c.   **Click Finish.**

d.   **Use the scroll and navigation bars to view all the data and pages.**

---

9.   **Close the preview window and close the report.**

     🖋 If you click Close on the Print Preview toolbar, then the Design view of the report will be displayed. Close that window as well.

a.   In the preview window, **click the Close button.**

b.   If necessary, **close rptMyDepartments.**

TOPIC C

Examine a Report in Design View

As with forms, there are generally improvements that can be made to reports. Imagine that you have been asked by users to alter the order and alignment of some of the report's controls and change the titles of some of the labels. In this topic, you will view the report in Design view and identify the sections that make up a report.

As with the form you created with the Form Wizard, the report you created can also be opened and viewed in Design view. A report is generally more complex to modify than a form.

Report Design View

If a professional presentation is your utmost consideration, then Design view may be the preferred report creation method. However, regardless of how a report is created, the layout of a report can always be modified in Design view. An existing report can be opened in Design view in three ways:

- You can right-click the report in the Database window and choose Design view.
- With the report selected in the Database window, you can click the Design icon.
- With the report opened in preview mode, you can click the View icon.

How to Examine a Report Displayed in Design View

Procedure Reference: Identify the Components of a Report in Design View

To identify the components of a report in Design view:

1. Select the report to examine.
2. Open the report.
3. Click the Design view button.
4. Examine the report.
5. Close the report.

ACTIVITY 6-3

Identifying the Components of a Report Displayed in Design View

Activity Time:

10 minutes

Setup:

The UseReports.mdb database is open.

Scenario:

Knowing that you will be called upon to customize reports, you've decided to spend a little time familiarizing yourself with how the report design determines final format. This way, you will be prepared to create a report.

What You Do	How You Do It
1. Open the rptDepartmentalInventory report, view all the pages, and then switch to Design view.	a. Double-click rptDepartmentalInventory.
	b. If necessary, **maximize the preview window.**

	c. **Use the navigation bar to view all pages.**
	d. On the preview window toolbar, **click Close.**
	e. **Open rptDepartmentalInventory in Design view.**

2. Where does the Report Header print?

    a) On the first page of the report.

    b) On the last page of the report.

    c) At the bottom of each page.

    d) At the top of each page.

LESSON 6

3. **What information is in the Report Header?**

   a) Name and Address

   b) Title and Date

   c) Page Number

   d) Date and Time

4. **What information does the Page Footer provide?**

   a) Date

   b) Time

   c) Name

   d) Page Number

5. **Determine which controls on the report are labels and which are text boxes.**

   🖈 You can move the property sheet by dragging it by the title bar.

   a. On the Report Design toolbar, **click the Properties button** 📇 .

   b. **Select the report title "Departmental Inventory" control.**

   c. **Observe the properties dialog box title bar.**

   🖈 This indicates that the control is a label that has been named Title.

   d. **Select other controls on the report and view the title bar of the properties dialog box.**

6. **Close the property sheet.**

   a. In the properties dialog box, **click the Close button.**

TOPIC D

Add a Calculated Field to a Report

To evaluate past and present business performance and make predictions on future business trends, the ability to perform calculations is often needed. These calculations can be included in reports. In this topic, you will add a control to produce a calculated field in your report.

Imagine that you have been asked to produce a report that displays a payroll total for the Research and Development department. You already have a report for this department that contains the salary amounts. By adding a control with a calculated field to your report you can easily produce the requested result.

The Toolbox

The toolbox is composed of design tools used to add controls to reports and forms. The same toolbox is used whether a form or report is being developed.

The Toolbox Icons

The following table displays most of the buttons in the toolbox.

Icon	Tool Name	Usage	Wizard
Aa	Label	Adds text only.	No
ab|	Text Box	Adds a graphical box that can contain fields, expressions, and text.	No
[xyz]	Option Group	Provides the user with option button choices, which are buttons that can take on a variety of formats, from round circles to large rectangular boxes.	Yes
	Toggle Button	A graphical button indicating a true/false or yes/no value.	No
	Option Button	This is similar to the option group, but each button operates independently. It can be used to designate true/false values, or multiple option buttons could be used to simulate an option group with multiple selections available.	No
	Check Box	A square graphic where a check mark represents a true value.	No
	Combo Box	A graphical box that can contain fields, expressions, and text with a drop-down arrow showing additional choices.	Yes
	List Box	A graphical box that displays all the choices available. It is similar to an option group but the record source can be text.	Yes
	Command Button	Used to place a button on the form, the button can be programmed to perform an action.	Yes

Icon	Tool Name	Usage	Wizard
	Image	Used to place a picture on the form or report.	No
	Unbound Object Frame	Used to place a variety of objects, including pictures, on a form or report.	No
	Bound Object Frame	This is used to place an OLE object on a form or report.	No
	Page Break	This inserts a page break wherever this control is placed. Using the Page Down key on a form will move the insertion point to the top of a page break. In a report, a page break will be inserted upon printing.	No
	Tab Control	The Tab Control places a graphical object on a form or report that positions data within pages accessed by a tab. Tab Controls are most often used in forms to maximize use of space.	No
	Subform (or) Subreport	This is used to place a subform or subreport on a form or report object.	Yes
	Line	This places a straight line on the report.	No
	Rectangle	This places a rectangular box on the report and can be used to cluster similar fields together or to enhance the graphical display.	No

How to Add a Calculated Field to a Report

Procedure Reference: Add a Calculated Field to a Report

To add a calculated field:

1. Open the report in Design view.

2. If necessary, display the Toolbox by clicking the Toolbox button.

3. In the Toolbox, click the Text Box tool.

4. Click the report design surface where you wish to place the calculated control.

5. Click in the text box control to place the insertion point.

6. Type an equal sign (=) and the formula for the calculation.

7. Press Enter or click away from the control.

8. Save the report.

ACTIVITY 6-4

Adding a Calculated Field to a Report

Activity Time:

10 minutes

Setup:

The rptDepartmentalInventory report of the UseReports database is open.

Scenario:

You've created the report for the Controller using the Report Wizard. Now the Controller would like you to amortize the cost of the computers over three years and include that calculation in the report. Adding a calculated field to the report will accomplish the amortization request.

What You Do	How You Do It
1. **Add a control containing an amortization formula.** Note that when you place the text box control, it contains the word Unbound. This is because you have not yet designated the contents of the control.	a. If necessary, on the Report Design toolbar, **click the Toolbox button** 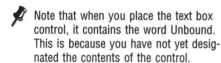 . b. In the Toolbox, **click the Text Box tool.** c. **Click in the Detail section to the right of the PurchasePrice control** to add the control. d. **Click in the text box control.** e. **Type = *[PurchasePrice]/3***

 The same techniques for selecting and moving controls used in the form design environment work in the report design environment. You can also move the Toolbox by dragging it by the title bar.

2. Delete the default label for the control, add a label with the caption *Amortized* to the right of the PurchasePrice heading, close the Toolbox, and preview the report.

   a. Click the default label control to select it.

   b. Press Delete.

   c. In the Toolbox, click the Label tool.

   d. In the LastName Header section to the right of the PurchasePrice label, drag to create the label control.

   e. Type *Amortized*

   f. In the Toolbox, click the Close button.

   g. Click the Print Preview button.

3. Save your report as *rptMyInventoryReport* and close the preview window.

   a. Save the report as *rptMyInventoryReport*

   b. Click Close to close the Print Preview window.

TOPIC E

Modify the Format Properties of a Control

You have added a control and a calculated field to your report and the resulting value is displayed in the report's output. You are not pleased with the default display of the value and wish to change it. By modifying the format properties of the control that performs the calculation, you can change the value's appearance.

Adding a control to a report can greatly enhance the output and the value it has to the organization. However, the default properties, such as the formatting of output, are not always what is appropriate. By modifying the format properties of the control, you can produce the desired presentation.

How to Modify a Control's Properties

Procedure Reference: Modify a Control's Properties

To modify a control's properties:

1. Open the report in Design view.

2. Select the control and click the Properties button, or right-click the control and choose Properties.

3. If necessary, in the property sheet, select the Format tab.

4. In the Format property box, from the drop-down list, choose the format you want.

5. Close the property sheet.

6. Preview the report to see the new format.

7. Save the report.

ACTIVITY 6-5

Modifying a Control's Properties to Change the Output's Display

Activity Time:

10 minutes

Setup:

The rptMyInventoryReport report of the UseReports database is open.

Scenario:

The amortized output format of the rptMyInventoryReport needs to be changed to currency.

What You Do	How You Do It
1. Change the format of the new calculated control to currency.	a. In the Detail section, select the control containing the formula you entered.
	b. On the Report Design toolbar, click the Properties button.
	c. Select the Format tab.
	d. From the Format drop-down list, select Currency.
	e. Click Print Preview.
2. Change to Design view. In the Report Header section, select the text box with the Now() function in its control source and, from the Format drop-down list, select the Short Date choice. Preview the report, and then save the report.	a. Switch to Design view.

b. In the Report Header section, **select the control containing the Now() function.**

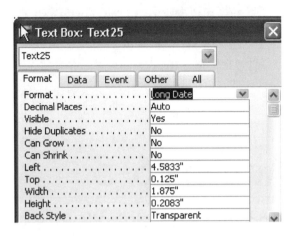

c. In the properties dialog box, from the Format drop-down list, **select Short Date.**

d. **Click Print Preview.**

e. **Return to Design view and save the report.**

TOPIC F

AutoFormat a Report

When you ran the Report Wizard, you probably noticed a list of styles that you could choose from. Wouldn't it be convenient if you could change from one report format to another without re-creating the entire report? The AutoFormat feature allows you to accomplish this. In this topic, you will examine the different AutoFormat reports available and apply your selection to a report.

Imagine that you have created a report that is to be used by several different departments in the organization. The contents of the report are just what they needed, but you have had several requests for different formats. This may seem to be a trivial matter, and you really don't wish to redesign the same report over and over. Using the AutoFormat feature, you can easily modify the report's format.

How to Apply an AutoFormat Style to a Report

Procedure Reference: Apply an AutoFormat Style to a Report

To AutoFormat a report:

1. Open the report in Design view.

2. Choose Edit→Select Report, or click the Report Selector.

3. On the Report Design toolbar, click the AutoFormat button.

4. In the Report AutoFormats list box, select the new format.

5. Click OK.

6. Preview the report to see the new style.

7. Save the report.

ACTIVITY 6-6

Applying an AutoFormat Style to a Report

Activity Time:

10 minutes

Setup:

The rptMyInventoryReport report of the UseReports database is open in Design view.

Scenario:

You are not pleased with the format of the rptMyInventoryReport report. You could attempt to adjust a number of properties and controls, but time is critical. There is another possibility—the AutoFormat feature may provide the solution.

What You Do	How You Do It
1. With no controls selected, **open the AutoFormat dialog box and choose a report format you like.** Then, **apply the format and preview the report.**	a. In the property sheet dialog box, **click the Close button.**
	b. **Click a blank area of the report** to deselect all controls.
	c. **Choose Edit→Select Report.**
	d. On the Report Design toolbar, **click the AutoFormat button.**

e. In the Report AutoFormats list box, **select the Bold format and observe the preview.**

f. **Preview each of the remaining formats and select the one you prefer.**

g. **Click OK.**

h. **Print Preview your report.**

2. **Switch to Design view. Save and close the report.**

a. **Switch to Design view.**

b. **Click Save.**

c. **Click the Close button.**

TOPIC G

Adjust the Width of a Report

There are times when a report contains so much information that the information to be displayed exceeds the size of the display area and causes blank pages to be printed in your report. In this topic, you will modify the margin settings to prevent this situation.

Imagine you have been asked to produce a lengthy report for an important business meeting. When you run and print the report, you find that every other page is a blank page. This is certainly not an acceptable format for the presentation. By modifying the report's margin values you can eliminate the blank pages.

How to Adjust the Margin Settings on a Report

Procedure Reference: Adjust a Report's Margin Settings

To adjust a report's margins:

1. Open the report in Design view.

2. On the horizontal ruler, note the width of the report.

3. Calculate left and right margin settings that, when added to the report width, are no greater than the width of the paper.

4. Choose File→Page Setup and enter the Left and Right margin values.

5. Click OK.

6. Preview the report to check your results.

7. Save the report.

ACTIVITY 6-7

Adjusting a Report's Margin Settings

Activity Time:

15 minutes

Setup:

The UseReports.mdb file is open.

Scenario:

You've spent a lot of time perfecting your report and sent it off to the printer. When you picked it up, every other page is mostly blank. Adjusting the margin settings will fix it.

What You Do	How You Do It
1. Print Preview rptFixMargins, viewing two pages side by side.	a. In the Database window, **right-click rptFixMargins and choose Print Preview.**
	b. On the Print Preview toolbar, **click the Two Pages button.**
	c. **Page down and examine the entire report.** The blank pages alternate between the printed pages.

2. Why are there blank pages between the printed pages?

   a) There is not enough text on the pages.

   b) The font is too large.

   c) The margin setting is too narrow.

   d) The margin setting is too wide.

---

3. In Design view, **note the width of the report. Open the Page Setup dialog box and notice the margin settings.**

   a. In Design view, on the horizontal ruler, **note the width of the report.** It is approximately 6.75 inches wide.

   b. **Choose File→Page Setup and note the margin settings.** Each margin is set to 1 inch.

---

4. Why are these settings causing the blank pages?

   What do you think your options might be for fixing this problem?

---

5. **Change the margins to eliminate the blank pages. Then, preview the report, save it as** *rptMyFixMargins*, **and close it.**

   a. In the Page Setup dialog box, **change the Left and Right margin values to 0.75.**

   b. **Click OK.**

   c. **Print Preview all pages of the report.** The blank pages have been removed.

   d. **Close Print Preview.**

   e. **Save the file as** *rptMyFixMargins*

   f. **Click the Close button.**

---

6. **Close the UseReports database and close Access.**

   a. In the Database window, **click the Close button.**

   b. In the Microsoft Access window, **click the Close button.**

Lesson 6 Follow-up

In this lesson, you created an AutoReport and used the Report Wizard to create a report. Then, in Design view, you customized the report by adding a calculated field, modifying the format properties of a control, using the AutoFormat feature to change the report's format, and adjusting the width of the report.

1. **What kinds of reports will you create for your data?**

2. **What uses can you think of for calculated fields in your reports?**

Follow-up

In this course, you explored the concept of the relational database and accomplished various tasks using the basic features and components of Access 2003. In addition, you worked with tables to store, modify, and report on data; you created new queries, forms, and reports; and you modified existing queries, forms, and reports. You have also begun to prepare for the more advanced Access courses and have completed the first step toward obtaining your Microsoft Office Specialist certification.

What's Next?

The *Microsoft® Office Access 2003: Level 1* course introduced you to the basics of the Access application and prepared you to go to the Element K course, *Microsoft® Office Access 2003: Level 2.*

APPENDIX A

Microsoft Office Specialist Program

Selected Element K courseware addresses Microsoft Office Specialist skills. The following tables indicate where Access 2003 skills are covered. For example, 1-3 indicates the lesson and activity number applicable to that skill.

Core Skill Sets and Skills Being Measured	Access 2003: Level 1	Access 2003: Level 2	Access 2003: Level 3	Access 2003: Level 4
Create Access Databases				
Creating databases using Database Wizard		2-1		
Creating blank databases		2-2		
Create and Modify Tables				
Creating tables using Table Wizard		2-3		
Modifying table properties or structure		2-4, 2-5, 2-6, 3-1		
Define and Modify Field Types				
Creating Lookup fields		3-3		
Changing field types		2-5		
Modify Field Properties				
Changing field properties to display input masks		3-2		
Modifying field properties for tables in Design view		3-1		
Create and Modify One-to-Many Relationships				
Creating and modifying one-to-many relationships		2-7		
Enforce Referential Integrity				
Enforcing referential integrity in a one-to-many relationship		2-7		

Core Skill Sets and Skills Being Measured	Access 2003: Level 1	Access 2003: Level 2	Access 2003: Level 3	Access 2003: Level 4
Create and Modify Queries				
Creating and modifying Select queries using the Simple Query Wizard	4-3			
Creating and modifying Crosstab, unmatched, and duplicates queries			2-1, 2-3	
Create Forms				
Creating forms using the Form Wizard	5-3			
Creating AutoForms	5-2			
Add and Modify Form Controls and Properties				
Modifying form properties	5-5, 5-6, 5-7, 5-8			
Modifying specific form controls (e.g., text boxes, labels, bound controls)	5-5, 5-6, 6-5	6-1		
Create Reports				
Creating reports	6-1, 6-2	7-1, 7-6		
Add and Modify Report Control Properties				
Adding calculated controls to a report selection	6-4	7-4		
Create a Data Access Page				
Creating data access pages using the Page Wizard				1-1
Enter, Edit, and Delete Records				
Entering records into a datasheet	2-2			
Find and Move Among Records				
Using navigation controls to move among records	2-1, 2-5			
Import Data to Access				
Importing structured data into tables			3-4	
Create and Modify Calculated Fields and Aggregate Functions				
Adding calculated fields to queries in Design view	4-5			
Using aggregate functions in queries (e.g., AVG, COUNT)	4-6			
Modify Form Layout				
Aligning and spacing controls	5-6, 5-7			
Showing and hiding headers and footers		6-1		

Core Skill Sets and Skills Being Measured	Access 2003: Level 1	Access 2003: Level 2	Access 2003: Level 3	Access 2003: Level 4
Modify Report Layout and Page Setup				
Changing margins and page orientation		7-5		
Aligning, resizing, and spacing controls		7-3		
Format Datasheets				
Formatting a table or query for display			1-4	
Sort Records				
Sorting records in tables, queries, forms, and reports	2-3	5-1, 7-1		
Filter Records				
Filtering datasheets by form		4-1		
Filtering datasheets by selection	2-4	4-1		
Identify Object Dependencies				
Identifying object dependencies			7-5	
View Objects and Object Data in Other Views				
Previewing for print		2-7		
Using Datasheet, PivotChart, Web Page, and Layout view	1-4		2-5	1-1, 1-3, 2-5
Print Database Objects and Data				
Printing database objects and data		2-7	1-4	
Export Data From Access				
Exporting data from Access (e.g., Excel)		8-3		
Back Up a Database				
Backing up a database			7-2	
Compact and Repair Databases				
Using Compact and Repair			7-3	

Notes

LESSON LABS

Due to classroom setup constraints, some labs cannot be keyed in sequence immediately following their associated lesson. Your instructor will tell you whether your labs can be practiced immediately following the lesson or whether they require separate setup from the main lesson content.

LESSON 1 LAB 1

Examining the Microsoft Northwind.mdb Database

Activity Time:

10 minutes

Data Files:

- Northwind.mdb

Scenario:

The consultant that installed your Access application and developed the company's databases has suggested to your manager that you practice using the program before actually working with the company's real data. He suggested opening and touring the Microsoft Northwind.mdb database, which comes as part of the application.

---

1. If necessary, **launch Access.**

---

2. **Search for and locate the Northwind.mdb database.**

---

3. **Open the Northwind database and display the Database window. Close the task pane.** At the Welcome screen, **click OK. Close the Main Switchboard.**

---

4. **Open the Customers table and examine the table in Datasheet view.**

---

5. **Examine the table in Design view.**

---

6. Close the table, and then close the database.

LESSON 2 LAB 1

Working with Data in Tables

Activity Time:

10 minutes

Data Files:

- UseForms.mdb

Scenario:

Imagine that you work as a data entry person for the GSC Corporation and you have just received a new customer's information. Before the customer can place an order they need to be added to the company's database. To add the customer, you need to open the UseForms. mdb database and input the necessary data.

1. In the UseForms.mdb database, **use the frmGSCCustomers form to add the following new customer data to the Customers table:**
   - CustomerID: *22000*
   - CustomerName: *Maple River Cleaners*
   - Address: *2 Sharp Stone Way*
   - City: *Hamlin*
   - Region: *MN*
   - Country: *US*
   - Postal Code: *56789*
   - Phone: *567 898 8800*
   - Fax: *567 898 8801*

2. **Close the form.**

3. In the tblCustomers table, **verify that the new customer's data was added correctly.**

4. **Close the table and the database; do not save your changes.**

LESSON 3 LAB 1

Examining the Northwind.mdb Database Relationships Window

Activity Time:

10 minutes

Data Files:

- Northwind.mdb

Scenario:

To reinforce your understanding of table links and relationships, the consultant also suggested that you examine the Northwind.mdb database's Relationship window and open several tables and subdatasheets to familiarize yourself with their use in a larger database environment.

---

1. **Search for and locate the Northwind.mdb database.**

---

2. **Display the Relationships window.**

---

3. **Right-click in the header of the Orders table and choose Table Design** to display the table in Design view.

---

4. **Display the table in Datasheet view.**

---

5. **Open several of the Customer record's subdatasheets** to examine the orders they have placed.

---

6. **Close the subdatasheets, close the table, close the Relationships window, and then close the Database window.**

LESSON 4 LAB 1

Creating and Modifying the Design of Select Queries

Activity Time:

15 minutes

Data Files:

- BookBiz.mdb

Scenario:

Imagine that you run a book bindery business. Your database includes tables that store information about each book, each order placed, and each customer. In this activity, you will create several queries to answer business-related questions, such as the following:

- Which books have sold?
- Which book orders have been for 250 or more books?
- How many sales transactions were recorded by the sales rep whose ID is EN1-22?
- Which transactions did sales rep EN1-22 have on August 16, 2001?
- How much did each individual book order cost?

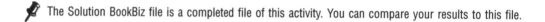 The Solution BookBiz file is a completed file of this activity. You can compare your results to this file.

1. **Open the BookBiz database.**

2. **Imagine that you would like to see a listing of which books have sold. Use the Query Wizard to display data from both the BookOrders and Books tables.** From the BookOrders table, add the SalesId, Date, and Quantity fields. From the Books table, add the BookNumber and BookPrice fields.

3. **Indicate that you want to see the Detail records.**

4. **Give your query the title of *MyBookSales***

5. **Run the query.**

6. Next, suppose you want to view only a portion of the records. First, you want to view all of the orders that were for a quantity of 250 or greater. **Use criteria to select just the records you want. Record the number of records that satisfy this criteria:** _____.

   You want to view all the records for the sales rep whose ID number is EN1-22. **Enter the appropriate criteria. Record the number of records that satisfy this criteria:** _____.

   Next, you want to know how many of the sales records for sales rep EN1-22 occurred on 8/16/2001. **Enter the appropriate criteria. Record the number of records that satisfy this criteria:** _____.

   Save your revised query as *MySelectBookSales* **and close it.**

7. Next, you'll create a query that answers the question, "How much did each individual book order cost?" **Create a query in Design view that includes the BookOrders table and the Customers table. Add the CustomerName, Quantity, and BookNumber fields to the design grid. Sort the query records by CustomerName. Run the query and view the results.**

8. **Return to the query's Design view and add the Books table to the query.** From the Books table, **add the Title field to the design grid.**

9. **Create a field that calculates the total price each customer owes for each book order. (Multiply the Quantity field from the BookOrders table by the BookPrice field from the Books table.) Change the default calculated field name to** *OrderCost*

10. **Run the query and, before closing it, save it as** *MyBookCosts*

11. **Close the BookBiz database.**

LESSON 5 LAB 1

Creating and Modifying Forms

Activity Time:

15 minutes

Data Files:

- BreadBiz.mdb

Scenario:

Imagine that you run a company that supplies bread mixes to gourmet and specialty shops. You want to create a data entry form that will make it easier to add new customers and refer to customer orders. You'll need to include customer information, as well as order details. Use the Form Wizard to quickly create a basic form and then modify the form you created.

 The Solution BreadBiz file is a completed file of this activity. You can compare your results to this file.

1. **Open the BreadBiz database.**

2. **In the BreadBiz database, use the Form Wizard to create a form based on the Customers and OrderDetails tables.** From the Customers table, **add all the fields to the selected field list.** From the OrderDetails table, **add all the fields to the selected fields list.**

3. **Specify that you want to view the information in the form by Customers.**

4. **Use the Datasheet layout. Choose a form style you like. Save the form as** *MyCustomers* **and save the subform as** *MyOrderDetails Subform*

5. **Customize the appearance of the form by selecting, sizing, aligning, and moving controls.**

6. **Save the modified form design and view the form.**

7. **Close the form and close the BreadBiz database.**

LESSON 6 LAB 1

Creating and Modifying Reports

Activity Time:

20 minutes

Data Files:

- PersonnelBiz.mdb

Scenario:

The PersonnelBiz database contains basic data about employees, compensation, departments, and parking lots. You want to compile some of this data into various reports. You will use the Report Wizard to create a phone list report based on a query. You will also work in Design view to make some modifications to a report that focuses on the employee payroll.

 The Solution PersonnelBiz file is a completed file of this activity. You can compare your results to this file.

1. **Open the PersonnelBiz database.**

2. In the upcoming days, the company parking lots are being repaved and you'll need to notify employees by calling them as necessary. **Use the Report Wizard to create a printed phone list report based on the ParkingLot query.**
   - Add the following fields: FirstName, LastName, ParkingLot, and Phone.
   - View your data by Employees.
   - Group the report based on the ParkingLot.
   - Sort by the FirstName field in ascending order.
   - Select the Tabular layout and Corporate style for the report.
   - Name the report MyPhoneList
   - Preview the report.

   Close the report.

3. Suppose you already created another report and want to complete it by enhancing its appearance. In EmployeePay report's Design view, **apply the Soft Gray AutoFormat** to change the look of the report.

4. You want to add a field that calculates the annual salary. Under the Annual Salary label control, **create a field that multiplies Weekly Hours, Hourly Pay Rate, and 52. Delete the default label for the control and align the text box control as necessary. Change the format of the new calculated control so that it prints the values in Currency format with zero decimal places.**

5. **Change the format of the text control in the Page Footer section that contains the Date function from Short Date to Long Date.**

6. Save the revised report as *MyEmployeePay*

SOLUTIONS

Lesson 1

Activity 1-1

1. **What are some examples of collections of data that you use in your personal life?**

    Answers may include a cookbook, a TV program guide, mail-order catalogs, and a household inventory.

2. **What are some examples of collections of data that you use in your job?**

    Answers may include personnel records, customer or vendor lists, and purchasing information.

3. **Which of the following is representative of a relational database?**

    a) Note card

    ✓ b) Library file system

    c) Index in a book

    d) Glossary in a book

4. **Which of the following is *not* an advantage of the relational database?**

    a) Flexibility

    b) Simplicity

    ✓ c) Redundancy

    d) Ease of management

    e) Power

Activity 1-2

4. **By default, which of the following toolbar options are activated when you launch the Access application?**

    ✓ a) New

    ✓ b) Open

    c) Save

    d) Cut

    ✓ e) Microsoft Office Access Help

    f) Undo

    g) Code

    ✓ h) File Search

Activity 1-3

4. Match the type of Access object with the description of the function(s) that it performs.

_b_	report	a.	Displays data for editing.
_d_	table	b.	Arranges data for printed output.
_c_	query	c.	Displays selected data.
_a_	form	d.	Stores data on a single topic.

Activity 1-4

4. What is the data type of the EmployeeID field in tblEmployees?

    a) Currency

    b) Date

    c) Number

    ✓ d) Text

5. What is the data type of the DeptCode field in the tblEmployees table?

    a) Currency

    b) Date

    ✓ c) Number

    d) Text

6. What is the field size of EmployeeID?

    a) 2 characters

    ✓ b) 4 characters

    c) 20 characters

    d) 20 digits

Lesson 2

Activity 2-1

2. How many fields are displayed in the form?

    Nine.

3. What field is highlighted by default?

    CustomerID.

4. How many records are in the table?

    Fourteen.

Activity 2-2

3. How many records are in the table?
    - a) 12
    - b) 13
    - c) 14
    - ✓ d) 15

Activity 2-3

4. How is the table sorted?
    - ✓ a) By OrderID
    - b) By ItemNum
    - c) By Quantity

Activity 2-6

2. Was it necessary for any of the tables to be open for the report to run?

    No.

6. Did the information that appeared in the report come from a single table?

    No. It came from more than one table.

7. Why was it possible for the report to draw information from more than one table?

    Because there is a field in both tables that can be related. This shows the benefit of using a relational database application such as Access.

Lesson 3

Activity 3-1

2. According to the Relationships window, how many tables are connected in this database?
    - a) One
    - b) Three
    - ✓ c) Five
    - d) Seven

3. How many tables have more than one link to them?

    a) One

✓ b) Two

    c) Three

    d) Four

4. How many have more than two links?

✓ a) One

    b) Two

    c) Three

    d) Four

5. In the Relationships window, to which table(s) is the tblNotes table linked?

✓ a) tblComputers

    b) tblDepartments

    c) tblEmployees

    d) tblManufacturers

    e) tblNotes

Activity 3-2

2. In tblDepartments, what type of key is DeptCode in the tblDepartments-tblEmployees relationship?

✓ a) Primary key

    b) Foreign key

    c) Primary and foreign key

3. In tblEmployees, what type of key is DeptCode in the tblDepartments-tblEmployees relationship?

    a) Primary key

✓ b) Foreign key

    c) Primary and foreign key

4. In the tblComputers-tblNotes relationship, in which table is AssetTag a primary key?

    a) tblComputers

    b) tblNotes

    c) Neither

✓ d) Both

Lesson 4

Activity 4-1

3. How many records are now displayed?

    a) 7

    b) 12

    ✓ c) 19

    d) 25

Activity 4-3

2. How many records are displayed?

    a) 11

    b) 21

    ✓ c) 23

    d) 32

7. How many records are displayed?

    a) 5

    ✓ b) 10

    c) 15

    d) 20

Activity 4-4

1. What is the answer to: 4 + (3 * 5)?

    a) 12

    b) 14

    c) 17

    ✓ d) 19

    e) 35

2. What is the answer to: (4 + 3) * 5?

    ✓ a) 35

    b) 12

    c) 19

    d) 17

    e) 60

Activity 4-5

3. **What is Rob Abbott's weekly pay?**

   a) 56

   b) 250

   ✓ c) 760

   d) 2,500

Lesson 5

Activity 5-1

1. **When designing a form, who should you keep foremost in mind?**

   a) Your boss

   b) Your co-worker

   ✓ c) The user

   d) The consultant

2. **In Design view, which section of a form would typically contain page numbering information?**

   a) Header

   b) Detail

   ✓ c) Footer

3. **Which of the Form Wizard layout styles shows multiple records per page?**

   a) Columnar

   ✓ b) Tabular

   ✓ c) Datasheet

   d) Justified

Activity 5-2

3. __True__ True or False? The number of fields in the form is the same as the number of fields in the table.

4. __True__ True or False? New records can be added to the table with the AutoForm you created.

7. __True__ True or False? The subdatasheet will expand if you click the plus sign (+) in the form.

Activity 5-5

2. **Which text box controls appear to be too small?**

   ✓ a) Address text box

   b) Postal Code label

   ✓ c) Postal Code text box

   d) Region label

Lesson 6

Activity 6-1

2. **What features does the printed datasheet have?**

   The name of the data source and the current date would be printed at the top of each page. The column headings would also be printed. The data is easy to read with each record arranged horizontally in a grid.

3. **What disadvantages are there to printing the query datasheet?**

   There are no totals, and there is no formatting. In addition, the data is split across two pages.

5. **How does the AutoReport compare to the printed datasheet?**

   The fields are arranged in a vertical column. An extra blank line separates each record. There's no heading, date, or page numbers. The report is eight pages long.

Activity 6-3

2. **Where does the Report Header print?**

   ✓ a) On the first page of the report.

   b) On the last page of the report.

   c) At the bottom of each page.

   d) At the top of each page.

3. **What information is in the Report Header?**

   a) Name and Address

   ✓ b) Title and Date

   c) Page Number

   d) Date and Time

Solutions

4. **What information does the Page Footer provide?**

    a) Date

    b) Time

    c) Name

    ✓ d) Page Number

Activity 6-7

2. **Why are there blank pages between the printed pages?**

    a) There is not enough text on the pages.

    b) The font is too large.

    c) The margin setting is too narrow.

    ✓ d) The margin setting is too wide.

4. **Why are these settings causing the blank pages?**

    The report is in Portrait orientation, which means the page is 8.5 inches wide. The report width of 6.75 inches plus 1 inch left and right margins exceeds this width and causes the blank pages.

    What do you think your options might be for fixing this problem?

    You could:

    - *Decrease the width of the lines and then decrease the width of the report in Design view.*

    - *Change the report to Landscape orientation.*

    - *Make the margins smaller.*

GLOSSARY

control
An object that is used to display data, allow user input, or perform an action.

data types
The allowable values that can be stored in fields.

database
A collection of related information or data.

expression
A combination of identifiers, operators, and values that produces a result.

field
A category of information that pertains to all records.

foreign key
A field in one table that links to a primary key in another table.

form
An Access object used to manage data in a table.

icon
A button with a representative picture on it.

prefix
A notation preceding an object name that indicates the object type.

primary key
A field or combination of fields containing a value that uniquely identifies a record.

query
An Access object that displays data from one or more tables in an ordered manner.

record
A set of data about one person or thing.

relational database
A database that stores information in multiple tables, and that can extract, reorganize, or display that information.

Select query
A query that retrieves data from one or more tables and enables you to ask questions about the data.

table
A group of records stored in rows and columns.

value
A single piece of data.

NOTES

INDEX

A

Access environment, 5
Access objects, 8
arithmetic calculation, 63
arithmetic operator, 61
  order of operation, 61
AutoForm, 72, 73
  creating an, 75
AutoFormat, 113
AutoReport, 96
  creating an, 96

B

Boolean
  See: conditional operator

C

calculated field, 63, 108
columnar form, 73
comparison operator, 56
conditional operator, 56
  adding to a query, 57
control, 82
  aligning, 88, 91
  modifying properties of a, 110
  moving a, 89
  selecting a, 82, 91
  sizing a, 85, 91
  spacing, 88, 91
Current Record Indicator, 12

D

data types, 13
database, 2
  opening, 9
  relational, 2
  viewing, 9
datasheet form, 73
Datasheet view, 12

Design view, 13

E

expression, 61
Expression Builder, 62

F

field, 2, 12
field name, 13
field properties, 13
filter
  removing a, 28
foreign key, 41, 42
form, 8, 18
  columnar, 73
  creating, 78
  creating a, 72, 73, 75
  datasheet, 73
  Design view, 74
  Detail section, 74
  Footer section, 74
  Header section, 74
  justified, 73
  modifying a, 91
  navigating in, 19
  tabular, 73
form control, 82
  aligning, 88, 91
  moving a, 89
  selecting a, 82, 91
  sizing a, 85, 91
  spacing, 88, 91
Form Wizard, 73
  creating a form, 78
  layouts, 73

I

icon, 5

INDEX

J

justified form, 73

L

logical operator
    See: conditional operator

M

margin settings, 115
menu bar, 5

N

naming conventions, 9
navigation bar, 12

O

objects, 8
order of operation, 61

P

prefix, 28
primary key, 41, 42

Q

query, 8, 27
  adding a calculated field, 63
  Select query, 50
Query Design toolbar, 51

R

record, 2, 12
  adding a, 22
  calculation on groups of, 67
  deleting a, 22
  sorting, 25
  updating a, 30
record selector, 12
recordset
  displaying a, 28
relational database, 2, 3
relationships between tables, 38
Relationships window, 38
report, 8
  adding a calculated field, 108
  adjusting the margins of a, 115
  AutoFormat a, 113
  components, 104
  creating a, 96, 98, 99
  Design view, 104
  modifying controls on a, 110
  running a, 33
Report Wizard, 98
  creating a report, 99

S

Select query, 50
  creating a, 53
selection conditions
  adding, 57
subdatasheet, 43
  collapsing a, 44
  expanding a, 44
  finding data in a, 44

T

tab order, 91
table, 2, 8
  relationships, 38
tabular form, 73
task pane, 5
toolbar, 5
toolbox, 107

V

value, 2

Your notes: _____

_____

_____

_____

_____

_____

_____

_____

_____

_____

_____

Your notes: _____

_____

_____

_____

_____

_____

_____

_____

_____

_____

_____

Your notes: _____

_____

_____

_____

_____

_____

_____

_____

_____

_____

_____

Your notes: _____

_____

_____

_____

_____

_____

_____

_____

_____

_____

_____

_____